W9-CHR-997

LOST WORLDS AND MYSTERIOUS CIVILIZATIONS

Pompeii

LOST WORLDS AND
MYSTERIOUS CIVILIZATIONS

LOST WORLDS AND MYSTERIOUS CIVILIZATIONS

Pompeii

Heather Lehr Wagner

CHELSEA HOUSE
An Infobase Learning Company

Pompeii

Copyright ©2012 by Infobase Learning

Chelsea House
An imprint of Infobase Learning
132 West 31st Street
New York NY 10001

Library of Congress Cataloging-in-Publication Data
Wagner, Heather Lehr.
  Pompeii / by Heather Lehr Wagner.
      p. cm. — (Lost worlds and mysterious civilizations)
  Includes bibliographical references and index.
  ISBN 978-1-60413-971-6 (hardcover)
  1. Pompeii (Extinct city)—Juvenile literature. 2. Vesuvius (Italy)—Eruption, 79—Juvenile literature. I. Title. II. Series.
  DG70.P7W32 2011
  937.7256807—dc22   2011011637

Chelsea House books are available at special discounts when purchased in bulk quantities for businesses, associations, institutions, or sales promotions. Please call our Special Sales Department in New York at (212) 967-8800 or (800) 322-8755.

You can find Chelsea House on the World Wide Web at http://www.infobaselearning.com

Text design by Erika K. Arroyo
Cover design by Alicia Post
Composition by EJB Publishing Services
Cover printed by IBT Global, Troy, N.Y.
Book printed and bound by IBT Global, Troy, N.Y.
Date printed: December 2011
Printed in the United States of America

10 9 8 7 6 5 4 3 2 1

This book is printed on acid-free paper.

All links and Web addresses were checked and verified to be correct at the time of publication. Because of the dynamic nature of the Web, some addresses and links may have changed since publication and may no longer be valid.

Contents

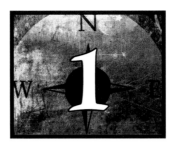

Victims
of Vesuvius

They faced the end of their lives in different ways. Some raced to the edges of the city, clutching treasured possessions or money. Some huddled together in an upper room, hoping that height might bring safety. Others, recognizing that they were dying, bowed their heads or curled up in the streets as the gases, molten rock, and volcanic debris swept over them.

More than 1,000 victims have been discovered in the ruins of Pompeii, forever trapped in that city when Mount Vesuvius erupted on August 24 in the year A.D. 79. The volcanic eruption that brought their doom also created an extraordinary method of preserving them so that, more than a century later, archaeologists exploring the ruins of Pompeii could simply pour plaster into the spaces created by the slowly decomposing bodies and clothing to re-create the victims, from the garments to the expressions on their faces. The same destructive cloud also preserved the streets of Pompeii, as well as portions of many of its homes and most important buildings, ensuring that future generations could look to this once relatively minor city in the Roman Empire to gain important clues about how life was lived in Italy nearly 2,000 years ago.

For the people of Pompeii, their final hours would have been terrifying. There were a series of minor earthquakes in the days leading up to the eruption of Mount Vesuvius. Earthquakes were nothing new to the people of Pompeii. In fact, their city had suffered a devastating earthquake on May 2, in the year A.D. 62, 17 years earlier. Many of Pompeii's most important structures had been rebuilt, but others were still under construction to repair damage from that earlier earthquake when Vesuvius erupted.

When Mount Vesuvius erupted in A.D. 79, approximately 2,000 people living in and around Pompeii died as a result of the natural disaster. The ash expelled from the volcano covered the city, preserving Pompeii and its citizens in their final moments of life.

The tremors were probably enough to prompt many people to leave their homes. Only about 1,100 bodies have been found in the ruins, in a city whose population was thought to have been nearly 20,000. While a portion of Pompeii (about a quarter of the ancient city) still has not yet been excavated, it seems likely that at least some of the city's citizens fled with their possessions when the minor earthquakes began.

Those who waited paid for the decision with their lives. Archaeological clues—where the people were in the city, what they were wearing, what objects were found near them—paint a picture of who these victims were. A family of four was found near the Forum, once the center of Pompeii's political and social activities. The father was at the front of the group. He was a large man, and he had pulled his cloak up around his face to help him breathe through the cloud of ash. He was carrying money, gold jewelry, and a few keys. He had probably locked up his home and possessions as the family raced to safety. Two small girls are behind him, and their mother is in the back. She, too, was carrying some treasured possessions: a mirror, some silver spoons, a pair of goblets, a medallion, and a small amber figurine. The mother had hitched up her long dress to make it easier for her to move quickly.

One of Pompeii's wealthier families remained in their home, determined to wait out the disaster with their slaves in the safety of the back rooms of the house. There they were found hundreds of years later—six adults and six children. One of the young women, adorned with jewels, was nearly nine months pregnant, and perhaps this is why the family chose not to risk a desperate flight to safety. She died near a nine-year-old boy who, DNA (deoxyribonucleic acid) evidence reveals, was probably her younger brother.

Many were clearly in the process of running for their lives when they were overwhelmed by the molten lava and ash. The bodies of 18 people and several dogs have been found in a single small room in the barracks that housed the city's gladiators. They likely hurried to the barracks when they realized they could not outrun the volcano's explosive force. A doctor or some kind of medical man has been found clutching his box of medical instruments in the large open space near the southern gates of Pompeii. A priest was discovered carrying some of his shrine's valuable items a short distance from the temple. A little girl has been identified, still clinging to her mother. A slave, his legs trapped by iron bands, had no chance of escape and his body was found in the garden of a large house in the center of Pompeii, undoubtedly the house where he had been a servant. A cloth worker's guard dog, firmly tied to a post in front of its owner's house, was also unable to escape.

DEATH NEAR THE TOMBS

The gates that lined the edge of Pompeii became the final resting place of many of its citizens well before Mount Vesuvius erupted. Tombs of Pompeii's wealthiest citizens—many of them elaborate memorials—marked the roads that led out of the city. As Vesuvius gave out what Mary Beard described in *The Fires of Vesuvius* as a "a deadly, burning combination of gases, volcanic debris and molten rock travelling at huge speed, against which nothing could survive," those attempting a final, desperate escape were cut down next to the tombs of Pompeians who had died from other causes years earlier.

Among those discovered near the tombs was a couple carrying only a small key and a bronze lamp in the shape of human head, a style of portable lamp popular in the first century. Oil was poured into a hole in the figure's forehead and the flame burned just below the mouth. A group of about 20 perished near the couple, although archaeological evidence from the buildup of layers of volcanic pumice suggests that this larger group died after the couple, probably after the first initial rain of volcanic rock seemed to have slowed. There were mostly young men in this group, one of whom carried a dagger, but the rest seemed to have been empty-handed.

The few women in the group, by contrast, all carried whatever must have been valuable and close at hand. For one, this was a small silver statue of the goddess Fortuna, ironically representing good luck, and several gold and silver rings. For others, these treasures included coins, keys, a jewelry case containing a necklace and earrings, silver spoons, and even a silver medicine box.

Many in this group were discovered, more than 1,000 years later, clinging to branches of wood. It is possible that, as the volcanic debris rushed toward them, they may have tried to climb the trees that lined the road in a final effort to save themselves.

These victims of Mount Vesuvius offer a poignant reminder that Pompeii, up until its final seconds, was a real town, a town of wealthy wine merchants and slaves, gladiators and temple priests, who were in the midst of busy, ordinary lives when the volcano erupted. Pompeii is often visited and studied to gain understanding of what life was like in the first century in the Roman Empire, but in fact Pompeii itself had only been part of the Roman Empire for less than 200 years. Conquered by Rome in 89 B.C., Pompeii's ruins contain evidence of this conquest, with older buildings constructed in the style of the Etruscans or Greeks, who had once dominated the region, standing next to traditional Roman structures and old and new homes.

Pompeii was, by most standards, an "old" city, more than 600 years old at the time of its destruction. Its largest and most expensive homes were in the north and west. In the southern portion of the city was the Forum, and to the east of the Forum were a series of crooked streets containing modest wooden homes where the tradesmen and artisans lived. Artesian wells, introduced with the conquest by Rome, brought fresh running water to

Pompeii (*foreground*) was a thriving ancient metropolis before Vesuvius (*background*) erupted, burying the entire city under a deep layer of ash. Pompeii was lost for more than 1,500 years, but its remarkable preservation has helped us understand life in the Roman Empire.

many Pompeians, and the city housed several elaborate bathhouses and theaters, including one theater near the southern part of the town that could hold about 5,000 spectators. Gladiator contests, a popular source of entertainment, were held in the Amphitheater.

Over time, cities expand or contract depending on the wealth and vitality of their citizens. Old buildings are replaced by new; homes are built or razed to reflect changing fashions and the needs of the population. It becomes harder and harder to discover the past, to understand the people of an earlier time and view their city as they had seen it.

The tragedy of Pompeii—the volcanic eruption that brought about the city's sudden end—has also become the means of its preservation. The city that once might have become a minor footnote in the distant past of the Roman Empire has instead become an important source of historical evidence, and a place where visitors can go to understand life in the first century. In the ruins of Pompeii, an ancient city endures.

Pompeii's Past

For several days the people of Pompeii had felt the earth shake, but they had become accustomed to periodic rumblings beneath the ground. Ignoring the warnings that something different—something devastating—was about to happen, the citizens of this bustling port town went about their business, unaware that tragedy was about to strike.

In that August in the year A.D. 79, Pompeii was still a town under construction. Significant sections and several buildings had been damaged after a major earthquake struck the region on May 2 in the year A.D. 62, and during the next 17 years efforts had been underway to rebuild or replace many of the city's central structures. A new bath complex had recently been completed, providing Pompeians with a place to gather and enjoy the comforts of a cold, warm, or hot bath, a massage, or a chance to gossip with neighbors.

Pompeii was more than 600 years old, and had been part of the Roman Empire for more than 160 years. Located on the southwestern coast of modern-day Italy, about 8 miles (13 kilometers) from Naples and 130 miles (209 km) from Rome, Pompeii had transformed over the years from a town built on trade to a vacation spot. With the beauty of the Bay of Naples to its west, feeding into the Mediterranean Sea, Pompeii was enjoying a growing reputation as a resort community, where wealthy Roman citizens built lavish, luxurious villas along the coastline, and spectacles and gladiator competitions attracted people from the surrounding communities, especially during the summer months.

Benefiting from its location—with the bay to the west and shielded by the Apennine Mountains on the east—Pompeii enjoyed a temperate climate. Part of the region known as Campania, Pompeii was in one of Italy's most productive areas. Sheep grazed in the mountains, two to three grain crops were harvested each year, and the region was famous as one of the principal producers of olives.

Because of its fertile soil and strategic location, Pompeii was targeted by many invaders during its 600 years. The precise date of the founding of a community there is not known, but estimates are that the first settlement was founded sometime around the eighth century B.C. This would have been a settlement of Oscans, one of the oldest groups of people who lived along the Italian peninsula. This group—the *gens pompeiana*, or people of Pompeii—was the first to use the name Pompeii to refer to their community. They are thought to have moved into Pompeii from the Apennine Mountains and gradually built homes there, cultivating cereal crops and herding sheep.

In that time, the region was still sparsely populated, and because of its location on the main route leading north and south and between the Mediterranean and the fertile territory further inland, Pompeii slowly developed into an important trading center. Archaeological evidence is gradually being discovered in the region that hints at what life might have been like during this period.

The Pompeians of this early era would have lived in horseshoe-shaped huts, each divided into an entrance, a living area, and a space for cooking. Some huts also had lofts for sleeping or storage and thatched roofs. Excavated pottery reveals that these settlers used plates and hourglass-shaped containers to store food items. Their diet included flour, grains, almonds, acorns, olives, and mushrooms—traces of all of these food items have been uncovered in archaeological digs. These ancient peoples raised goats, sheep, cattle, and pigs.

What is particularly fascinating about these prehistoric people is the archaeological evidence that suggests that they, too, experienced a cataclysmic eruption from Mount Vesuvius, thousands of years before the eruption that destroyed Pompeii. In December 1995 Italian archaeologists first uncovered the skeletal remains of a woman, thought to be about 20 years old, and a man in his mid-40s. Both bodies had their hands placed

Evidence of prehistoric civilizations occupying the area near Vesuvius indicates that the volcano had erupted and killed centuries before Pompeii ever existed. Stories of the ash, fumes, and lava that spewed from Vesuvius's crater (*above*) faded from memory as the volcano remained inactive.

over their faces, in a final effort to shield themselves from the force that had killed them.

A HISTORY FORGOTTEN

Stephen Hall, writing in the September 2007 issue of *National Geographic*, reports that archaeologists have used uncovered clues to reconstruct much about this eruption that took place in 1780 B.C. As Vesuvius began to erupt, and volcanic rock and small bits of pumice began to rain down, the couple described earlier probably fled their village along with many other people seeking safety. Traces of footprints, perfectly preserved for centuries in the volcanic ash and mud, show that in the panic villagers headed in many different directions. Those who headed north or northwest by chance or luck chose the safer path. Others, like the couple whose remains were discovered in 1995, headed east, up a gently sloping hill to a forest where undoubtedly they thought they might find safety.

The region, not far from the present-day Italian town of Avellino, some 18 miles (29 km) from Naples, quickly became buried under 3 feet (1 meter) of fiery rock and pumice. The eruption blocked out the sun, making it impossible to see more than a few feet ahead and gradually making breathing impossible. The couple fell about halfway up the hill and were soon covered by layers of pumice that ultimately preserved them, in the same poses they held when they fell to the ground, for approximately 3,780 years.

Vesuvius would have signaled the coming eruption first with earthquakes, then with a loud roaring force that shot superheated rocks, cinders, and ash up into the stratosphere. In this eruption, known as the Avellino eruption, scientists speculate that the force was so great that the rocks, cinders, and ash were propelled approximately 22 miles (35 km) high, a distance three times higher than the cruising altitude of commercial airplanes. The frightened people would have heard the noise and seen this huge plume of smoke rise up from the volcano's mouth where, because of the sheer force of the explosion, the plume would have lingered for several hours until it collapsed.

Quickly, a toxic "rain" of volcanic ash and small rocks, 1 to 2 inches (2.5 to 5 centimeter) wide, began to fall. The rocks were a combination of light pumice and harder stones known as *lapilli*, falling on the helpless people below at a speed of 90 miles (145 km) per hour. Next came a boiling avalanche of volcanic debris shooting out of the volcano. For those close to Vesuvius, this surge brought instant death. According to the *National Geographic* article, superheated winds, moving at speeds up to 240 miles (386 km) an hour, raced out from the volcano at temperatures up to 900°F (482°C), hot enough to boil water 10 miles (16 km) away. Those who escaped this initial blast were quickly choked by the clouds of volcanic ash in the air. Eight inches (20 cm) of this volcanic ash can cause modern roofs to collapse, but the area 3 miles (5 km) from Vesuvius was blanketed in ash 65 feet (20 m) deep during the Avellino eruption. Even 15 miles (24 km) from Vesuvius, the volcanic ash was 10 inches (25 cm) thick.

There were no written records to document this tragic eruption. Those who survived undoubtedly shared stories of the horrors that occurred when Vesuvius erupted, but gradually, over the generations, the stories disappeared and the descriptions of the clues that led to the eruption faded away, long forgotten some 2,000 years later, when once more a toxic plume shot up into the sky from the mouth of Vesuvius.

EARLY INFLUENCES

Eventually, settlers returned to the region. The volcanic ash nourished the soil, and the land once again was fertile. Its waterways provided Pompeii with an important role as a trading center for merchants, many of whom were Greek. The Greek presence gradually grew in Pompeii as Greek traders brought in goods to sell to the Oscans and exported the goods they received in return.

Gradually, as more and more Greeks moved into Pompeii, they began to extend what had once been principally a farming community (centered around the area that would eventually become Pompeii's Forum) into more of a prosperous commercial center. Greek influence would be felt in the architecture and art of Pompeii long after it had become part of the Roman Empire.

For a time, the Greeks and Etruscans fought for control of Pompeii and the other towns that lined the Bay of Naples. The Etruscans, a neighboring powerful group that also sought control of the seas for trade, managed to hold Pompeii for about 50 years before the Greeks finally recaptured the city around 474 B.C. The Greeks then fortified Pompeii's defenses by building walls around the city, traces of which still can be seen in Pompeii's ruins.

Years passed by without any volcanic activity, and Pompeii began to thrive as a popular resort destination and a commercial hub. Because it was located near the sea and surrounded by fertile land, marauders and other civilizations would target Pompeii for its riches and resources.

Pompeii's fertile land and prime location next drew the interest of the Samnites, a tribe of fierce and skilled warriors who spoke Oscan and lived in the mountainous regions of southern Italy. Unlike most of the residents of Pompeii, who made their living in trade or farming, the Samnites were fighters, equipped for combat and prepared to battle to the death in order to win the rich lands of Campania, and Pompeii was quickly conquered. Many structures in Pompeii show signs of the Samnite influence, and their use of building materials like volcanic rock and tufa, a type of limestone.

The Samnites' goal was to ultimately conquer all of the people of the Italian peninsula and set up a series of states that they would rule. It is inevitable that they would ultimately clash with the leaders of Rome, who were in the process of attempting the very same thing. A series of wars, known as the Samnite Wars, took place between 373 and 290 B.C.

Pompeii's involvement in the wars began in 310 B.C., when a Roman squadron sailed into the Bay of Naples and began moving up the Sarno River toward Pompeii. The Roman admiral, Publius Cornelius, ordered his soldiers to seize the town and they did, plundering its wealth and terrorizing its citizens. Pompeians responded by fighting back, gradually pushing the invading force out of the town. But in 20 years the Samnites were finally defeated and Pompeii fell under Roman control.

Pompeii was named as an "ally" of Rome, meaning that Pompeii kept its own language (which was Oscan) and its own culture but was forced

LUCIUS CORNELIUS SULLA

The Roman general Sulla was known for being a brutal conqueror, expanding the Roman Empire and enslaving people as he seized their lands. Regions that challenged Rome's authority or resisted conquest were often burned to the ground. But the Campania region around Pompeii benefited from Sulla's mercy; he loved the area, first encountered during a military campaign, and he built a home there.

Sulla was born in 138 B.C., not as wealthy as many others who aspired to a career in Roman politics but gifted with cunning and skill. An inheritance gave him just enough money to buy an important position in the Roman Senate, and successful military campaigns in North Africa and in the region we now know as Germany added to his prestige. He was placed in charge of Cilicia, an area that today encompasses parts of modern Turkey and Cyprus. Later, during the Social War in which provinces rebelled against Roman control, he successfully stamped out the rebellions, enslaving much of the population that had fought against Rome.

It was the next campaign that sparked trouble. Sulla had been given command to lead Roman forces in a war in territory that today forms part of Greece and Turkey. He had been appointed to the post by the Roman Senate, but at the last minute one of Sulla's rivals used violence and bribery to have the appointment withdrawn and himself named commander.

to submit to Roman authority without its people being given the benefits of Roman citizenship. It was an uncomfortable and difficult situation, and it inevitably led to struggle and revolt. In 90 B.C., Pompeii joined forces with several other cities that had also been forced to accept their status as "allies" of Rome, and the Social War for freedom began.

Rome gathered together its more experienced armies under the command of several brilliant generals to exert its authority over the rebellious provinces, but for two years first one and then the other side claimed victories. Finally, in 89 B.C., the Roman general Sulla established control over

Sulla learned of this just as he was preparing to depart for the region. Instead, surrounded by many of the men who had fought with him in the Social Wars, he marched on Rome, declared his rival and those who had supported him to be enemies of the state, and forced them to flee the city. He then reclaimed his command and headed for Greece. After successful military campaigns that claimed vast stretches of Greece for Rome, Sulla learned that another rival in Rome had decided to form his own army, possibly as a way to ensure that Sulla did not become too powerful. Sulla decided that the time had come for him to take his legions and once more march on Rome.

After fierce fighting, Sulla's forces seized control of Rome, and in late 82 B.C. he was named dictator of the empire. Up until then, the Roman policy had been to rule through the Senate, avoiding giving any one man too much power. Sulla's dictatorship marked the beginning of concentrating power in the hands of a single individual, a precedent that would eventually lead to the rule of emperors.

Sulla successfully executed many of his enemies, labeling them enemies of the state. He further consolidated his power by expanding the number of members of the Senate, appointing men who would be loyal to him. But in 79 B.C., he stepped down as dictator, expressing his belief that he had successfully restored Rome to its "traditional values." He retired to his home near Pompeii, where he died about a year later.

the region of Campania and Pompeii was once more part of the Roman Empire. Sulla gradually became ruler of Rome. Many of the cities he had conquered were razed as punishment for their rebellion, and their citizens made slaves. But Sulla, like many other Romans who would follow him, was captivated by the beauty of the Campania region. He built a lavish villa for himself not far from Pompeii and spent his final days there.

Rome took steps to build the peace in Pompeii. Its people were granted Roman citizenship. But they were also forced to make way for a significant new group: colonies of army veterans who were given land and ordered to build homes and settle there, all while keeping the peace. The patron saint of this new region would be the Roman goddess Venus, the goddess of love and beauty.

Life in a Roman Town

Under Roman rule, Pompeii once again began the process of transforming, this time from strategic port to vacation destination. As soldiers returned to Rome from Pompeii, they brought with them stories of the beauty of the countryside. Other Romans traveled to Pompeii to see firsthand the town they had heard about. Many of them chose to stay in the region, either permanently or else building elaborate villas to use as vacation homes.

Gradually, a prosperous middle class began to develop in Pompeii, made of merchants and tradesmen who built businesses catering to the needs of the wealthy Roman aristocracy. Luxury goods were manufactured or imported. Artisans specializing in fantastic decorations, elaborate fountains, and detailed mosaics plied their trade.

The city limits of Pompeii had expanded under the Samnites, and it was the Samnites who had enclosed the city in massive walls stretching for 2 miles (3 km). The center of Pompeii occupied approximately 165 acres (66.7 hectares) when the Romans first arrived, and the city, while it transformed under Roman rule, did not grow much beyond the limits first marked by the Samnites. The changes and transformations that took place for the next 350 years occurred largely within those massive walls.

Roman rule brought with it the elaborate system of organization and modernization that marked so many Roman cities as the Roman Empire flourished and spread. Traffic—pedestrian traffic and the traffic of carts and carriages pulled by horses, donkeys, and cattle—was brought under control with newly marked streets and footpaths. This is clear from the Porta Marina, the ancient gate that marks the entrance to Pompeii. Two archways stand side by side and mark the gate—one considerably wider and taller than the other. The smaller one, on the left, is the one that was intended for pedestrians. The one on the right was designed for animals and the carts that carried people into the city and transported salt and fish from the sea. The footpaths were raised up from the road to ensure that pedestrians could move freely about the city even if rain had flooded the streets.

One of the chief architectural achievements that marked the Roman Empire was its ability to harness and channel running water, ensuring that homes were provided with a constant supply. Each building in Pompeii had its own water tank, designed to capture rainwater from the roof. The Romans also built an aqueduct in Pompeii, which supplied water to the public fountains, public baths, and to the wealthiest residents.

As many Pompeians prospered under Roman rule, and as wealthy Romans moved into the city, many of the more humble and modest homes in the city began to disappear. In some cases, two adjoining homes would be converted into a single, larger structure. New shops and businesses opened. The ruins of Pompeii reveal the gradual shift in construction— older homes were made of limestone and homes built after the Roman occupation were made from stone or, later, brick.

AT HOME IN POMPEII

While the homes in Pompeii varied depending on when they were built and the wealth and status of the owners, there was a basic floor plan common to many of them, which has revealed much about typical homes built during this time. Unlike many modern cities and towns, there were not separate and distinct residential districts and commercial districts in Pompeii. Instead, Pompeian merchants and tradesmen lived behind their shops.

The architecture of these homes was designed to ensure privacy and maintain separate areas for working, living, and entertaining. Shops and workshops were located on the outside of the house, facing the street, and with separate entrances for customers. In Pompeii, these included *thermopolium*, a kind of café that sold hot drinks; *pistrinum*, a mill and bakery; *fullonica*, a laundry service that bleached garments like togas and offered pressing and dyeing; and *caupona*, a tavern or inn.

If you entered the separate entrance for a Pompeian home, you might be met by the home's *atriensis*, the servant who was the doorman and caretaker.

Immediately beyond the entranceway you would step into an atrium with a large pool in the center. This pool was designed to catch rainwater falling from an opening in the roof above, which also let in light and ensured that those stepping into the home were greeted with a bright, airy space.

Small bedrooms—*cubicula*—were located next to the atrium. Larger homes might also have a second story, which would be reached by stairs placed at the side of the atrium. Just beyond the bedrooms and behind the atrium would be the living room, followed by the dining room. Pompeians reclined on couches while they dined, rather than sitting on chairs, so the dining room would be equipped with several (generally at least three) couches placed around a low table.

Beyond the dining room, many Pompeian homes opened onto a garden. The garden might contain fountains, statues, and sometimes a

Houses in Pompeii provided both a home and a business to its inhabitants. Shops, bakeries, and cafes faced the street and customers had a special entrance, separate from the private home of the owners. Above, the ovens of a bakery in Pompeii.

space where vegetables were grown. Next to the garden was the kitchen, equipped with a pantry and oven, and the servant's quarters.

Wealthier Pompeians enjoyed even more space. These more elaborate villas often contained private bathing areas with rooms for bathing at different temperatures—hot, tepid, and cold. These homes might also have separate areas exclusively for the use of the women of the family, and additional living space. There might be a second, larger garden designed more for entertaining, with fountains shooting jet sprays of water, pools of colorful fish, statues of gods, and space to dine out of doors, as well as living rooms that opened onto the garden. These homes also had a separate entrance designed for the use of servants and tradesmen.

These larger homes were designed to impress visitors and surprise guests. As you moved deeper into the home, the noise and bustle of the street would be left behind. The beauty of the gardens, the soothing sound of the fountain, the art and statues that decorated the home were all intended to convey a message about the status and wealth of the owner. Guests, in turn, would clearly understand their own status and importance by how far into the home they were ushered. Those with a message or a bit of business to conduct often remained close to the entrance; favored friends would move deeper into the heart of the home to dine or enjoy the beauty of the garden.

THE WRITING ON THE WALL

As part of the Roman Empire, Pompeii fell under the authority of the emperor, but like many Roman colonies day-to-day governing was in the hands of a type of city council. Four public officials belonged to two different categories: two Duumviri Iuri Dicundo, the officials responsible for administering laws, and two Aediles, who were responsible for streets, buildings, and markets. There were other public officials, Quinquennales, elected to a one-year term every five years, whose job was to count the population, much like our modern census officials.

Citizens of Pompeii voted in the districts where they lived; candidates who received the majority of the votes won the election. Only certain men could vote. Women, children, slaves, and gladiators could not, but they participated in elections by publicizing their support for one candidate or another. They did this in the form of graffiti scrawled on Pompeii's walls and buildings in charcoal, red chalk, or with some sharp tool. This graffiti

A popular feature in Pompeian homes was an atrium. These rooms were open spaces with a pool in the middle to catch rainwater from an opening in the roof. Wealthy citizens were known to have spacious atriums filled with decorations and art. Above, the atrium inside a Pompeian politician's home.

has survived, containing messages urging the support of one particular group for a particular candidate. In the thousands of examples that survived, we can see messages of support for candidates from groups, including farmers, mule drivers, ballplayers, porters, carpenters, innkeepers, fishermen, bankers, barbers, jewelers, shoemakers, and dyers. The tradition was to erase the messages once the election was over, and scrawl new messages in their place during the next election, so the messages preserved in Pompeian ruins are most likely from an election that took place in that final year.

In the ancient world of Pompeii, graffiti was not considered to be damaging property. Instead, it was a common form of writing, one that was often interactive, with one person beginning a story, joke, or poem and others adding to it as they passed by.

In addition to campaign messages, there are other forms of graffiti in Pompeii, some containing jokes, instructions, love notes, and drawings. Helen Tanzer, in *The Common People of Pompeii*, notes that the graffiti shows the concerns, amusements, and humor of Pompeii's ordinary citizens. Thousands and thousands of examples of graffiti have been discovered in Pompeii, so many in fact that one example ironically states, "Everybody writes on the walls but me," while another remarks, "I'm amazed, O wall, that you have not fallen in ruins, you who support the tediousness of so many writers."

Graffiti in Pompeii has revealed that Emperor Nero was quite popular. Many messages are scrawled simply wishing happiness to all of Pompeii. There are simpler, more familiar types of graffiti, such as "Satura was here on September 3rd" and "Marcus loves Spendusa." On the wall of the gladiator barracks was the message "Celadus the Thracian gladiator is the delight of all the girls." There are jokes, vulgar comments, and more practical messages, almost like contemporary posters and notices: "The city block of the Arrii Pollii in the possession of Gnaeus Alleius Nigidius Maius is available to rent from July 1st. There are shops on the first floor, upper stories, high-class rooms and a house. A person interested in renting this property should contact Primus, the slave of Gnaeus Alleius Nigidius Maius."

Messages that have survived for centuries show clearly what life was like in Pompeii before Vesuvius erupted. The streets were full of ordinary people who urged support for a candidate, declared their love, and promoted their businesses. In the days and weeks before Vesuvius erupted, Pompeii was full of people focused on their lives, and the messages they left behind give us a picture of what it was like to live in the first century.

ROMAN CIVILIZATION

By that first century A.D., the Roman Empire occupied vast stretches of land, not only in Italy but throughout most of the territories we know today as Europe, northern Africa, and significant portions of the Middle East. The triumphant Roman army, which had expanded the empire, now was charged with keeping the peace and guarding the thousands of miles of frontiers. Soldiers settled into the regions, like Pompeii, that they had once conquered, becoming part of the community. When they retired, they were given grants of land or money. They often then married local women.

Roman society was divided into different groups or classes. Pompeians had been granted Roman citizenship when the territory was conquered. Other residents of Rome's provinces were not so fortunate, but could earn

POMPEII GRAFFITI

Many examples of ancient Roman graffiti have been uncovered on the walls of Pompeii. Written in Latin, this graffiti was not viewed as vandalism, but instead as an acceptable means of communication. Graffiti served as want ads, political advertisements, and a kind of message board for jokes, instructions, and comments.

The Web site www.pompeiana.org lists many examples of the graffiti uncovered in Pompeii, including the following, excerpted below:

"Epaphra is not good at ball games."

"On April 19th I made bread."

"Postpone your tiresome quarrels if you can, or leave and take them with you."

"Gaius Sabinus says a fond hello to Statius."

"Blondie has taught me to hate dark-haired girls."

"If anyone does not believe in Venus they should gaze at my girlfriend."

"A copper pot went missing from my shop. Anyone who returns it to me will be given 65 bronze coins. 20 more will be given for information leading to the capture of the thief."

"A small problem gets larger if you ignore it."

"The man I am having dinner with is a barbarian."

"Drinks: 14 coins; lard: 2 coins; bread: 3 coins; three meat cutlets: 12 coins; 4 sausages: 8 coins."

"Pyrrhus to his colleague Chius: I grieve because I hear you have died; and so farewell."

"Gaius Pumidius Dipilus was here on October 3rd 78 B.C."

citizenship for themselves and their families after 25 years of service to the empire. Members of the citizen class enjoyed certain privileges that were denied to noncitizens. Even within the citizen class there were divisions. The chief administrators of Rome—the consuls, magistrates, and provincial governors—were all members of the senate. Senators were members of the elite group that governed Rome under the direction of the emperor, and were chosen by the emperor. The next rank of citizens was the equestrians, the highest class of military officers, wealthy enough to provide and care for their own horses. Slaves, most often from conquered territories but also enslaved as a legal punishment or by being born to slave parents, were brought in to provide the labor that built and maintained the empire.

But, through faithful service or hard work, it was possible to move up to a different level within Roman society. Slaves could earn their freedom and eventually become citizens. Gladiators were slaves who could win their freedom through success in staged combat held in Rome's arenas. Equestrians could become senators.

Typical Roman men wore knee-length, sleeveless tunics, rather than trousers. Women wore an inner and outer tunic of wool or linen, depending on the temperature. The wealthiest men and women wore garments made of imported fabrics, such as Indian cotton and Chinese silk. In cooler temperatures both men and women wore cloaks, and on formal occasions both men and women wore heavy white togas, fashioned with brooches or *fibula* at the shoulder.

All Roman cities had a large public space with public buildings placed around it. This was called the forum. Government business would take place in one of the buildings there, markets would be held there, and the arenas for public entertainment were generally nearby.

For most wealthy Roman children, their earliest years were spent in play and school. Girls received only a basic education, if any, as their principal task was thought to be managing the home. There were a few jobs available to women—they might run a small business or become a midwife, helping with the birth of children. Wealthier families hired tutors for their sons, to prepare them for a career in government or law. Schooling generally began at age seven, and the local schools ran from dawn until noon; children spent a lot of time memorizing, learning to write on a wax tablet, and calculating using an abacus. But school was reserved for the more prosperous members of the community; poorer children and children of slaves received no education and instead were expected to work.

In a household in Pompeii you might have found slaves cleaning, cooking, and performing various tasks, members of the family working or entertaining guests. There would have been animals—guard dogs, cats used to keep away rats and mice, caged birds, and other typical family pets. The Pompeian household generally had a shrine to the Roman gods; each family claimed particular gods that were their personal protectors, and they would spend time worshiping at the family shrine each day. This household shrine was called the *lararium*, and several examples have been found in the ruins of Pompeii.

Homes were lit with oil lamps made of bronze or pottery. They burned olive oil. The lamps were often elaborately designed, and different styles of lamps came in and out of fashion, including lamps shaped like animals and lamps shaped like human heads. The homes had very little furniture. There might be beds and couches for dining, a few small tables, possibly a cupboard or strong box to hold valuables.

Wealthy homes had a connection to the aqueduct that also supplied water to public areas. There were bathhouses where society gathered not only to clean themselves but also to exercise and to socialize, as well as public fountains from which Pompeians could gather water for use at home. Lead pipes, depending on an elaborate system that took advantage of gravity's force, carried water to fountains, and also carried away sewage from public toilets. Examples of these toilets have been uncovered—rows of seats carved out of stone, with a water trough below designed to carry away waste. According to Simon James in *Ancient Rome*, the Romans used sponges on sticks instead of toilet paper.

ENTERTAINMENT

As Pompeii developed into a vacation destination, a place for summer homes and a luxury retreat for wealthy Romans, entertainment became increasingly important. People from nearby communities would travel to Pompeii for a day of fun and pleasure. Some forms of entertainment would be familiar to us today. The Romans enjoyed theater. The tradition of theater had begun with the Greeks, and Romans copied the basic form of plays, which often involved wealthy women who had been kidnapped by evildoers, old men who were generally foolish, and slaves that were cunningly plotting against their masters. Roman audiences preferred comedies to tragedies, and most plays had happy endings.

Romans also developed new forms of performance. They introduced audiences to a kind of comedy called mime. Unlike modern mimes, the mimes of Roman times involved actors speaking. Mime was considered a lower form of entertainment, and there were usually stock characters in every mime, one of which was a foolish character named Stupidus. Romans also developed the pantomime, in which an actor would dance and act out a story from Greek mythology or legend while being accompanied by music and singing. In mimes, men and women performed without masks, but in other forms of Roman theater the roles were all played by men, often wearing elaborate masks designed to show the audience the type of character they were portraying, whether male or female, young or old, hero or villain. Theater performances, like many other forms of entertainment, were often sponsored by wealthy men wishing to gain popularity with the people, and so admission was free.

Romans also enjoyed horse racing. In the Roman races, horses pulled their riders (generally slaves) around an arena in elaborate chariots. Chariots were pulled either by two or four horses; in a single race there might be up to 12 chariots making seven laps around an arena (a distance of about 5 miles [or 8 km]). It was a dangerous sport, especially when the horse and chariot had to navigate a turn, and crashes and injuries happened all the time. The horses and riders were grouped into different teams, and people would bet on their favorite team, cheer for their favorite rider, and buy snacks. The largest racetrack in the Roman Empire, the Circus Maximus in Rome, could seat up to 250,000 people.

The threat of death and injury that hovered over the racetrack was nothing compared to other violent sports that took place in the coliseum or arena. One of the greatest forms of entertainment for Roman citizens was watching men facing wild animals or each other in a fight to the death. Gladiators were trained for this brutal sport—a successful gladiator, usually a slave, might earn his freedom with enough victories in the arena. Exotic animals (antelopes, lions, tigers, rhinoceroses, and bears) were brought in from the farthest reaches of the Roman Empire to fight each other, to kill defenseless criminals, or test the skill and courage of the gladiators. In other competitions gladiators would face off against each other, fighting to the death. Arenas and coliseums were constructed

Roman cities like Pompeii had a special arena for gladiator fights. Held in a large coliseum, spectators in the stands would watch and cheer as men battled wild animals or other gladiators to the death.

with mazes of cells and chambers below where the animals and gladiators waited their turn in the arena. Hidden elevators and trapdoors opened at the right moment, and the ground of the area was covered in sand to absorb the blood of those killed. (The arena in Pompeii was built earlier and did not have these underground chambers. Instead, animals and gladiators were brought in from various entrance points around the arena on ramps.)

Gladiators were trained in special schools to prepare them for the fights. They often attracted fans, and many specialized in a particular weapon or type of combat. One type was the *retiarii*, the "net men," who were equipped like particularly fierce fishermen. They used a weighted net to catch or trip their opponents, and then a large trident (modeled after that used by the god Neptune) to stab.

These types of entertainment would go on all day. In the morning, wild animals would fight each other or kill criminals, then there would be a break for the bodies to be removed and fresh sand to be spread. The main attraction—the gladiators—came in the afternoon. Several pairs of gladiators might fight in the arena at the same time. If wounded, a gladiator could appeal for mercy to the emperor or whichever public official had sponsored the entertainment. Then it was up to the crowd. If they indicated by their cheers and applause that the gladiator had fought well enough to be spared, he would live to fight another day. If not, a downward jab of the thumb showed the gladiator that he was about to die.

THE PUBLIC BATHS

Bathing was very different in the Pompeii of Roman times. Only the very wealthiest citizens had places to bathe in their homes. Most citizens went to the public baths, not simply to clean themselves but to meet friends, gossip, relax, or exercise and play games. There were separate bathing spaces for men and women.

Surrounding the baths were halls or exercise yards. Here Pompeians could train with weights or play games. One game involved catching colored balls of different sizes, from tiny, light balls to large, heavy medicine balls. Others might play board games or gamble with dice. In the hall there was usually a shaded area where people could sit and enjoy snacks and drinks sold by vendors.

The bathhouses were accessed through changing rooms, where people would strip off all of their clothing and place them on shelves. Next came a series of rooms, each hotter than the next. There were dry heat rooms, much like a sauna, and steamy rooms where Pompeians would sweat to clean their pores. Instead of soap, Pompeians used olive oil to clean their bodies. Next they would plunge into a cold bath or swimming pool, and then have a massage.

The bathhouses were heated by fires outside, kept burning by slaves. According to *Ancient Rome*, the bathhouses were designed so that hot air from the fire could travel under the floors of the bathhouses and through hollow tiles in the walls to chimneys in the roof. This hot air was so strong and heated the rooms so thoroughly that Pompeians walking through these hot chambers had to wear clogs to protect their feet from burning.

For the wealthier citizens of Pompeii, there were plenty of opportunities for work and play. The Roman conquest had brought many decades of peace, and little thought was given to the mountains looming in the distance.

The People
of Pompeii

The ruins of Pompeii have revealed much about the people who used to walk the streets, live in the buildings, and carve messages on the city's walls. There were wealthy citizens who built lavish villas as primary or secondary residences; there were prosperous businessmen, ambitious politicians, gladiators, and slaves. Of the estimated 20,000 who lived in Pompeii at the time of the eruption, half were children. Like most ancient people, Pompeians were shorter than modern humans. The average woman was about 4½ feet (1.4 m) tall and lived to be 39 years old. Men were a few inches taller and generally lived to be a few years older—the average life expectancy for men was 41 years.

Many different workers provided goods and services for the people of Pompeii. Pompeii was particularly known for two products—its woolen cloth and *garum*, a sauce made from fish used in Roman cooking. Its strong taste could be used to disguise meat or fish that might not be very fresh, and it was bottled and traded in markets and shops, along with olive oil and wine.

One of the largest groups of shop owners in Pompeii were the fullers, who provided a cleaning and dying service for cloth and garments. Fullers used tubs filled with water or, some reports have suggested, urine as a kind of astringent to clean garments. The cloth or garments were placed in large tubs and then slaves stepped on the cloth to push it back down into the liquid and move it around, a human version of the agitating action done in modern washing machines. The garments were then spread over a large frame to dry, and finally put through a wooden press to smooth them out.

Wealthy Pompeians could afford to have artists decorate the walls of their villas with intricate frescoes depicting everyday life. Many of these frescoes survived the volcanic eruption, providing archaeologists with a glimpse into the lives of Pompeians. From the work above, we can learn much about women, children, and slaves.

Because Roman citizens, male and female, were required by law to wear white togas for public occasions, fullers were kept busy keeping the togas clean and white. Several fulleries have been found in the ruins of Pompeii. One of them is attached to a private home. Its foundations show that three tubs were once in place for washing the clothes, large enough for several slaves to tread on the garments. There were also three large basins made of masonry, designed to soak and rinse garments, and a place where the press would have been fixed to provide the final ironing. Paintings on the wall of this fuller's shop showed the steps in this business of cleaning and dyeing garments.

In Pompeii, cloth was dyed using a variety of natural substances, including sumac wood from Venice, which dyed garments purple. New cloth could be dipped into colors, and older or faded garments could be brought in for dyeing to freshen the colors.

Archaeologists have uncovered the business belonging to Vecilius Verecundus, who manufactured woolen cloth and items made from felt—things like slippers, gloves, and hats. Ribbons and linen garments were also for sale in this business, and he would not only sell new clothing items but also buy back old ones and redo them for resale.

Near one of the gates into Pompeii—the Stabian gate—archaeologists have uncovered the remains of a tannery. Leather goods were brought here for processing. The ruins include oblong basins lined with wood and 15 deep masonry pits, also used during the tanning.

Graffiti found on the walls of Pompeii gives additional clues to the merchants and tradesmen who populated the city. There were linen weavers and merchants, tailors, a vendor of capes designed for poorer people or soldiers, shoemakers, and cobblers, or shoe repairers.

Bakers formed another large group in Pompeii. More than 20 bakeries, or *pistores*, have been uncovered in the ruins of Pompeii. Bread formed an important part of the Roman diet, and bakers also served as millers in Pompeii, grinding the grains as well as producing baked goods. Peasants did not have their own kitchens, so they would either buy hot food from a vendor or bring food to the bakery, where it could be heated on the large, hot ovens there.

In ancient Pompeii, the largest part of a bakery would be set aside for milling, or grinding, the grain. Large mills were placed with enough space around them so that they could be turned by donkeys. A bakery would also have a stable nearby or attached to it to house the donkeys that provided labor to turn the heavy mills.

A bakery would also have a kneading room, an oven, and a space for storing the bread once it had been baked. Slaves providing the human labor were also given sleeping quarters nearby.

According to Helen Tanzer in *The Common People of Pompeii*, the mills were made of local lava. Yet another Pompeian business involved manufacturing millstones used to grind the grain and exporting them to other parts of the Roman Empire. The lower part of the millstone was cone shaped and fitted into a heavy base with a raised edge. Here, in this base, was a kind of trough where grain fell once it had been ground. The upper part of the mill was shaped like an hourglass. Grain was poured into the top, slid down the cone, and then was trapped between the two stones. The distance between these top and bottom millstones could be adjusted to create a finer or coarser grain. A wooden frame was placed around the sides of the upper part of the mill, to which donkeys could be attached by chain or collar to turn the stone. In some cases, slaves rather than donkeys were used, and this was considered to be a particularly brutal form of labor, often a punishment for slaves whose masters were dissatisfied with their work.

The baking part of the operation required building a large fire in an oven. Once the oven had reached the right temperature, the ashes were then raked out and the bread put inside. The oven was closed once the bread was inside. The hot oven would cool off as the bread baked, so that by the time one batch was finished and the bread removed the process had to be done all over again.

Bread was actually baking in the ovens when Pompeii was destroyed, and the fossilized remains of these loaves have been uncovered to give us a clue of what ancient bread actually looked like. In Pompeii, the custom was to mark or shape the bread into eight wedges. The bread was flat and round. Bakers would mark their bread with their name. Bakeries also produced rolls, small flavored breads similar to biscotti, and even pastries. Wealthy citizens would sometimes sponsor a free distribution of bread to the poor as a way to earn good will or increase their popularity prior to an election.

FOOD FOR THOUGHT

Pompeians could buy their food—both raw and cooked—in shops, in the public market, or from street vendors. There were also special markets designed for the sale of fruits and vegetables—the Porticus Pomariorum and Forum Olerum in Pompeii. Saturday was the main market day in Pompeii. Fruit sellers were particularly plentiful, and cherries, figs, grapes, and dates were a common part of the local diet. Beans, either cooked or soaked and sprinkled with salt to eat as a snack, were plentiful, as well as garlic, onions, and leeks.

Signs in Pompeii indicate that vendors sold many different grains, including wheat, semolina, barley, and bran. Pompeians could buy poultry, pork—principally in the form of ham or sausage—mustard, and goat or sheep's milk. There was also fish, olives, and wine, all locally produced. Wine from the slopes of Mount Vesuvius—known as *vinum* Vesuvinum—was exported to other parts of Italy; one writer from that time, Pliny, critically noted his feeling that Pompeian wines often gave him a headache.

Because of the fertile land and the proximity of the sea, wealthy Pompeians could enjoy a variety of foods, particularly during the warmer months. But it is important to remember that modern cooking methods are quite different from those in ancient Rome, and homes did not have refrigerators or other methods of preserving foods for days or weeks.

Many of the foods we traditionally associate with Italian cooking did not exist in ancient Rome. Pasta had not yet been invented. Tomatoes did not exist, nor did potatoes—these would not be introduced into Europe until they were discovered in America. A typical diet was based on bread, beans, lentils, and perhaps a small amount of meat or fish. Most Roman citizens, even the wealthiest, ate very little during the day, and had only one large meal in the late afternoon: *cena,* or dinner.

Spices, herbs, and sauces—particularly the Pompeian fish sauce called *garum*—were used in most cooking, especially to disguise the taste if the meat or fish being served was not completely fresh. Wealthy Pompeians had cooks who prepared more elaborate meals that focused more on

Bread was a staple in the Pompeian diet, and many bakeries milled their own grain for their products. The volcanic eruption preserved everything in Pompeii, including the bread that was still baking in the ovens.

carving and serving the food in unique and artistic ways, rather than producing huge quantities of food.

In wealthier homes, there would almost always be guests for a meal, and so entertainment sometimes accompanied the food. Dancers might perform between courses, or there might be a reading of poetry.

Pompeians ate their dinner while reclining on large couches, designed to hold up to three people. The food and jugs of wine were placed on low tables and eaten without utensils. Finger bowls filled with water were often provided between courses so that diners could wash their hands. The dishes and jugs used to serve the food conveyed a message about the wealth of the owner. The wealthiest Pompeians served their food on beautiful, richly colored and decorated glass plates, while more ordinary citizens used Samian pottery, colored a glossy red and made into cups, plates, and bowls. Depending on the wealth of the host and the importance of the guest, wine and water would be served in jugs made from silver, bronze, glass, or pottery.

Some meals were designed to surprise guests, either with unusual ingredients or elaborate presentation. Records of meals and even recipes have survived from this time, and *Ancient Rome* notes that a meal might include dormice (a type of wild rodent) cooked in honey and poppy seeds, or songbirds served with quail eggs and asparagus sauce.

AWAY FROM HOME

The streets of Pompeii were lined with several different places to eat or rest. There were shops similar to modern wine bars, where you could drink and eat a small meal. There were inns with dining rooms, places that specialized in the sale of hot beverages, and places similar to takeaway shops where food could be bought to take home or eaten there. This would often be stews or soups that could be prepared in advance, kept hot for several hours, poured into bottles or jars, and taken home for reheating. For the poorest Pompeians, there were also *popinae*, which were places that sold the meats left over following an animal sacrifice to the gods. This was operated by a kind of butcher, who assisted the priests at animal sacrifices, where the choicest morsels were offered to the gods. The leftover bits could then be sold after the sacrifice had ended.

There were several inns in Pompeii, most of them located at or near the gates to the city. Merchants would travel into Pompeii, stay at the inns, and then deliver orders or sell their goods. Large, heavy carts and wagons were not allowed in the interior streets of Pompeii, so merchants often brought their goods into Pompeii, stabled their horses or donkeys at the inn, and then hired drivers to take them into the city in smaller carts—the equivalent of our modern taxis.

The wealthiest and most prominent travelers to Pompeii would stay at the homes of friends, or at their own villas, so the inns were designed for

DINING IN ANCIENT ROME

In ancient Rome, people generally ate lightly, consuming whatever was in season and available as there were few opportunities for storing food. These foods varied depending on the region (citizens closer to the sea would have had access to fish, for example) and by the wealth of the citizen. In cities like Pompeii, most food was purchased; some homes had small gardens that could produce vegetables, but most fruits and meats were purchased in the markets or shops. Wealthier citizens obviously enjoyed a more varied and plentiful diet.

For these citizens, breakfast would generally have meant bread or biscuits made of wheat. These would be dipped in wine or honey. Breakfast might also include olives, raisins, or some cheese.

Many citizens skipped lunch, since the largest meal of the day, *cena*, or dinner, was served in the late afternoon. Those who did eat a light meal around the middle of the workday would generally eat something cold, perhaps bread, fruit, some salad greens, or some cold foods leftover from the previous day's large meal.

The final meal of the day generally consisted of three courses, and it was eaten while reclining on couches set around a low table. The first course was a kind of appetizer, things like salad greens, mushrooms, eggs, or sardines. The second course was a main course, generally fish, poultry, or pork served with a vegetable. The third course was the dessert course, which was usually fruit, nuts, or small cakes sweetened with honey. Most Romans drank wine with their meals; it was usually mixed with water.

humbler citizens. Graffiti left on the walls around inns recorded the names of people who stayed there. There are many comments, some critical and some filled with praise, for the food and drink served at an establishment. One piece of graffiti—perhaps as a kind of ancient advertisement—noted that the ham prepared at the inn was so tasty that guests licked the pot or dish after eating the ham. There are drawings of hungry travelers and thirsty people holding out glasses for wine or water. One drawing shows guests being served by young women, although most servers in these drawings are boys. One piece of graffiti lists the prices of various types of wine, while another warns travelers, according to *The Common People of Pompeii*, "You can eat bread at Pompeii, but at Nuceria you will drink."

OTHER PROFESSIONS

The graffiti found in Pompeii's ruins mentions many other trades and professions, some listing the craftsman by name, others by the candidate for office they were promoting in the upcoming election. Shops offered goods made locally or on the premises, as well as items brought in by traders and salesmen from other parts of the empire.

Pompeii's craftsmen included goldsmiths and jewelers. Both men and women wore rings made from gold, silver, or other precious metals. Equestrians wore a special gold ring to show their rank in Roman society, and other rings with special carved stones in a unique mark would be used to seal important documents. Some rings were used as charms to protect the wearer from bad luck. Women also wore bracelets, necklaces, and earrings—many Pompeian women had pierced ears—as well as fancy brooches to fasten their togas or other garments. Most jewelry was made from inexpensive bronze or glass; wealthier women would have jewelry made from gold or silver or fashioned out of precious stones like sapphires or garnets. There were also engravers who specialized in carving designs or messages on precious objects.

Barbers also existed in Pompeii—one such shop is thought to have been located near the Stabian Baths. Men in Pompeii in the years just before the eruption wore their hair cut relatively short and their beards trimmed. There were also vendors specializing in perfumes and cosmetics. Perfumes generally contained olive oil and herbs or flowers with special scents. Most women wore makeup. In ancient Rome a pale complexion was prized for women, and Pompeian women would have achieved this look by putting powdered chalk or white lead on their faces. Cheeks and lips were given a rosy glow using red ocher, while ash was used in mixtures to make up eyes. Many of the materials used in these ancient cosmetics are now known to be poisonous.

Other craftsmen manufactured goods from copper or bronze, or shaped pottery from clay or glass. Peddlers sold pots and dishes in the markets or streets. Many everyday items were also made from animal bone. Butchers provided animal bones to these craftsmen, who would then carve them into combs, needles, pins, knife handles, and sword hilts, or game pieces and dice. There were woodworkers, carvers, and scriptors, whose job was to carve the formal announcements (generally in capital

Graffiti was another source of information for archaeologists studying Pompeii. Scrawled on walls and columns, the graffiti mentions citizens by name. The sample above shows an advertisement for a political campaign.

letters) on walls or buildings as well as write letters and documents for those who were illiterate.

Most ordinary people were illiterate. Books were rare and expensive. They had to be copied by hand, generally onto scrolls (books with pages were introduced late in the Roman Empire). While several different languages could be heard in the streets of Pompeii, Latin was the chief language used for speaking and writing in trade, government, and formal communication. The Latin alphabet, the alphabet still used in most Western nations, contained only 22 letters at the time—*I* and *J* were not separate letters, but different ways of writing the same letter; the same was true for *U* and *V*, and there were no *W*s or *Y*s. Writing was carved into stone, placed on wax tablets, printed onto scrolls made from papyrus, or scratched onto pots and pottery.

Pens were made from reeds or metal, and ink was made from a mixture of fine soot and water. Ordinary writing was put on wax tablets made from melted beeswax that could be wiped clean and reused, or on cheap, thin pieces of wood. Legal contracts were made from papyrus—paper made from reed fibers. The finest documents and books—generally precious religious texts—were written on vellum, sheets of very thin goatskin or lambskin, which was extremely expensive.

The streets of Pompeii thrived with business and trade. A tour though the ruins of Pompeii reveals a city bustling with enterprise at the moment of its destruction.

Walking the Streets of Pompeii

The buildings that once graced Pompeii are now in ruins, but in their shadows, the city still exists. You can walk through those ruins, studying the remains of different structures, and learn much about this city of 20,000.

It was a crowded city, with the inhabitants pushed together into an area measuring about 36 acres (14.5 ha) and surrounded by a 2-mile-long (3-km-long) wall. It would have been very hot in August; most of the residents would have spent as much time as possible in the interiors of their homes, near their gardens or fountains.

A visitor to the city would most likely have entered through the Porta Marina, one of the ancient gates. There were six original gates into Pompeii—Porta Marina, Porta Stabia, Porta Nuceria, Porta Sarno, Porta Nola, and Porta Vesuvio. Porta Marina, the entrance used by tourists today, is located in the southwestern section of the city. Two arches mark the entrance to Porta Marina, the smaller one for pedestrians and the larger for carts and animals.

To the right of that gate are the remains of a temple to Venus, Pompeii's patron goddess, which was in the process of being built when the city was destroyed. The original temple had been destroyed in the earthquake that struck Pompeii in A.D. 62; the new temple was intended to be larger and more elaborate than the original.

Near the gate were several warehouses, designed to store goods being brought into or out of the city. Several luxury homes were built near this gate, large villas designed to benefit from the views of the mountains and sea in the distance. One of these villas, now known as the Suburban Villa of Porta Marina (archaeologists gave names to many of the structures as they were excavated), had been partially destroyed during the earthquake in A.D. 62; it was being rebuilt at the time that Vesuvius erupted. The villa had a long porch, or colonnade stretching in front, with 43 columns and spectacular views of the mountains and water. Next to the porch was a large garden, and the villa had several living areas and the largest dining room in Pompeii, measuring 20 by 30 feet (6 x 9 m), and decorated with hand-painted panels on its walls.

Walking into Pompeii on the Via Marina, you come to the Forum, one of the key commercial, religious, and public spaces in the city. There were several important buildings around the Forum. There were government offices, where public officials met and carried out business, and a Comitium, a meeting place for the citizens of Pompeii where elections were held. There was the Basilica, the oldest public building in Pompeii, built between 120 and 78 B.C. In pre-Roman times the Basilica served as a covered market, but by the first century A.D. it was the home of Pompeii's courts. The Basilica was designed to impress; it consisted of three joined wings and an open courtyard in the middle. There were 28 columns lining the three wings of the Basilica, each more than 3 feet (1 m) in diameter and 32 feet (10 m) high, and the main entrance to the Basilica contained five doorways.

Also in the Forum were temples to the chief gods of the city, including temples for Apollo, Jupiter, Emperor Vespasian (it was believed that emperors could become gods after their death), and a more general space for other gods of the city (Sanctuary of the Lares). The fullers had a building that served as the headquarters for their guild near the Forum, and there was also a large food market.

On the other side of the Forum was the main commercial street of Pompeii, the Via Dell'Abbondanza. From dawn until late in the afternoon, this street was crowded with merchants, shoppers, slaves running errands for their masters, and people hurrying to and from their workplaces and homes. Homes lined either side of the Via Dell'Abbondanza, with shops opening onto the street and the living spaces tucked behind. You could buy food or hot drinks, bring clothing to be cleaned, or find a skilled craftsman all along this street. The walls of the buildings on either side were covered with graffiti, offering critical comments on the services offered inside the shops or proclaiming their support for a particular political candidate.

The main forum in Pompeii is one of the oldest areas of the city and was once surrounded by shops, public offices, and temples. One of the main gods of the city, Apollo, had his temple in the forum (*above*), from which you can see Vesuvius in the distance.

The Via Dell'Abbondanza ran nearly the entire length of Pompeii, from northeast to southwest. Not only did it serve as the access road to Pompeii's commercial district and to the Forum; it also led to the principal areas of entertainment in the city.

FINDING ENTERTAINMENT

A large area in the eastern part of the city, between the Porta Sarno and Porta Nuceria, or Sarno and Nuceria gates, houses Pompeii's Amphitheater and Large Palestra (a Greek term referring to a public space for athletic competition). The Amphitheater was built in 80 B.C., around the time Pompeii became a Roman colony. It was designed to be large enough to provide seating for Pompeii's entire population—20,000 people. Unlike many Roman amphitheaters, the one in Pompeii had no underground areas, and the structure was dug out so that much of the area lay below ground level.

The lowest seating area—the seats closest to the action—were reserved for dignitaries. The highest gallery was reserved for women and had its own stairs and entrances. Spectators were protected from sun and rain by a giant canopy, suspended over the arena with poles tucked into stone rings at the top of the Amphitheater.

The Amphitheater was used for sporting competitions, gladiator contests, and battles with wild animals. People came from miles around Pompeii to attend events in the Amphitheater. People from different towns often cheered for different teams or competitors. During one gladiator competition, in A.D. 59, a fight broke out between men from Pompeii and men from the nearby town of Nuceria. The fighting was so fierce that several men were killed and even more injured. The Roman Senate was so appalled at the violence that all spectacles were banned at Pompeii's Amphitheater for 10 years.

Next to the Amphitheater was the Villa of Julia Felix, which stretched across two building lots. Julia Felix lived on the property and also rented bathing facilities to out-of-town visitors and first-floor apartments for leases of five years.

Also next to the Amphitheater was the Large Palestra. Measuring 448 by 416 feet (136.5 by 127 m), this served as the location for the city's athletic competitions and exercises. The Palestra was completely surrounded by a large wall and equipped with a sizeable latrine at its southeast end. In the middle of the Palestra was a large swimming pool with steps on one side for entering the water. The swimming pool was surrounded by two rows of trees. A message uncovered on one of the western columns of the Palestra has suggested that a small community of Christians (who would have been persecuted during the Roman era) were living in Pompeii around the time of its destruction.

In the south-central section of Pompeii, near the Porta Stabia, was the Large Theater, dating from the end of the third century B.C. It was later enlarged, and an upper seating area and special boxed seats were added over the side entrances. As in the Amphitheater, the seats in the very front, closest to the stage (in an area we might call the orchestra pit today), were reserved for Pompeii's elite. The seats extended in rows in a half circle facing the stage; the Large Theater could seat more than 5,000 people. A canopy could also be placed over the seating areas to protect the audience from the elements. The theater itself was built of stone, but the stage was made of brick. Instead of a false or painted backdrop, performances took place in front of an elaborate facade decorated with columns and two stories of statues on pedestals and fountains gushing water.

Audiences at the Large Theater might enjoy comedies, interpretations of Latin works by Plautus and Terence, or versions of Greek plays by Euripides. The most popular were the more humorous skits that poked fun at heroes, often using risqué jokes and gestures.

Near the Large Theater was the Small Theater, or Odeon, a theater covered by a pyramid-shaped roof that was built in 80 B.C. Here Pompeians might attend a musical performance, dance, or pantomime. Behind the two theaters was a large, rectangular courtyard where the audience could mingle during intermissions. By A.D. 62 this courtyard had been transformed into barracks for the gladiators performing at the Amphitheater. Rooms were built on two floors circling the courtyard, and a kitchen was built in one area. Archaeologists found many different types of weapons used by gladiators in excavations of the ruins here.

TEMPLES FOR WORSHIP

The theater district of Pompeii also was the site for several temples. Pompeians, like many Romans, selected individual gods that had particular meaning for them. All Pompeians were expected to offer sacrifices to the official gods of Rome, such as Jupiter, the king of the gods, to Venus, the patron goddess of Pompeii, and to the god selected as the guardian for whichever emperor was in power. Juno, Jupiter's wife, was the patron goddess of women. Minerva was the goddess of wisdom and handicrafts, while Dionysus was the god of wine, and Mars was the god of war. There were gods thought to protect the home, and other gods who promoted healing.

Some Pompeians chose to worship foreign gods, particularly those thought to offer hope for an afterlife. Mithraism was a Persian cult that

Via Dell'Abbondanza, Pompeii's main street, was located next to the forum and was the commercial heart of the city. People could buy and trade anything on this thoroughfare, which almost ran the length of the city.

gained popularity in parts of the Roman Empire, particularly in the military, because of its focus on the struggle between good and evil, but it was a religion that welcomed only men. Isis was an Egyptian goddess whose worship became very popular in Pompeii; she was a goddess of fertility and motherhood and it was believed that she was able to create or destroy life through certain spoken words. Many different forms of worship were tolerated, with the exception of Christianity. As noted in *Ancient Rome,* because Christians would not offer sacrifices to the Roman gods, they were thought to be dangerous unbelievers whose refusal would offend the gods and endanger the empire. For this reason they were imprisoned and often put to death (sometimes in the arenas).

Near the theaters were temples for Jupiter and Isis. The Temple of Isis was destroyed in the earthquake of A.D. 62. It was then ordered rebuilt by N. Popidius Celsinus, a political official elected to office despite the fact that he was only six years old! Archaeologists uncovering the temple centuries later discovered the remains of a sacrifice on one of its altars. The temple had a large atrium, a room where members of the cult would meet, and rooms for the temple's priests. Because Isis was an Egyptian god, the temple also held a cistern or well that contained water from the Nile.

There were several public baths in Pompeii. The smallest and most elegant were the baths located near the Forum. These baths were intended to be used by people who came to the city from outside Pompeii, and were built shortly after Pompeii fell under Roman control. There were dressing rooms; areas for bathing in cold water, warm water, and hot water; and a large basin where visitors could wash their hands and faces with hot water. There were separate sections for men and women, and the entire complex was heated with hot air that circulated under the floor and came from a large fire furnace.

The Stabian Baths, with a main entrance on the Via dell'Abbondanza, were the oldest baths in Pompeii and the largest, built when the Romans first arrived in Pompeii. The men's bathing area was at the right; the women's area and the heating section were in the center. The men's dressing room was covered by a vault containing beautiful stucco artwork, and there were large marble benches and niches to place clothing near the entrance. These baths also had a gymnasium area, where Pompeian men could swim and then engage in sports like boxing. There was an open-air pool measuring 31 by 25 feet (9 by 7 m), which was 4 feet (1 m) deep. The women's area had two separate entrances, and their area for bathing in cold water was located in the dressing room. Separating the men's and women's hot-water bathing areas was the large heating section, which contained a giant furnace heated by fires, and three large cylindrical boilers designed to contain warm, hot, and very hot water.

Yet another bathhouse was placed at the intersection where two main city streets—Via di Nola and Via di Stabia—intersected. The baths were built shortly after the earthquake in A.D. 62, and as a more modern bath complex copied many of the contemporary techniques used in the Roman Empire. There were more open spaces, and features designed to let in more light. There was even a special extra-hot space designed for "sweating," much like contemporary saunas. This complex was still being completed at the time of the eruption; the swimming pool had not yet been finished.

WHERE THEY LIVED

Many homes have been uncovered in the ruins of Pompeii. Large and small, richly decorated or designed for practicality, they reveal much about the owners and their lives in this city. This trip through the streets of Pompeii concludes with stops at a few of these homes.

In some cases, archaeologists have been able to uncover clues that reveal the name of the owner of a few of the homes in Pompeii. In other cases, names have been given to the homes based on a statue or piece of art or other symbol discovered there.

One of the latter is the House of the Faun, named for the statue of a faun discovered in the home's ruins. The home is large and obviously belonged to one of Pompeii's wealthier citizens. Alberto Carpiceci, writing in *Pompeii: 2000 Years Ago and Today*, suggests that it probably belonged to Publius Sulla, the nephew of the Roman general who conquered Pompeii. Certain features of the home, including the steps at the entrance, suggest that it was a home for a particularly distinguished citizen.

The House of the Faun occupies an entire city block. It has two atriums—one for the main part of the house and another to the right with columns in the middle and an entrance to a separate part of the house, which may have been intended for the use of guests. There are two large gardens. The main atrium was decorated in richly colored marble and open to the sky above; in the central area there were a row of columns, the green garden, and the marble statue of a dancing faun in the center.

There is evidence that artwork was displayed in several areas of the home. An impressive mosaic stretched across the floor of one of the main living areas, which depicted a battle between Alexander the Great and the Persian king Darius. There were several dining spaces, including one outdoors and a space for dining in the colder winter months, all with their own mosaics. One mosaic depicted what seems to be a scene from the Nile, with a crocodile, hippopotamus, ducks, snakes, and birds interacting in the water. There were separate quarters for guests and servants, a stable for animals, spaces for a gardener and doorkeeper, and a bathing area.

The House of the Vettii was a slightly more modest home, thought to have been owned by two wealthy merchants, Aulus Vettius Restitutus and Aulus Vettius Conviva. The home was decorated in an expensive style designed to show the wealth of its owners. It was a two-story home, with

The House of the Vettii (*above*), a two-story structure with two atriums and a garden filled with topiary and fountains, reflects the wealth of its owners. The home was also richly decorated with red panels, paintings, and murals.

the women's quarters located on the upper floor. The entrance to the home was decorated with several pictures and murals of gods designed to provide continued success and ward off envy from visiting guests. The home contained a small kitchen, two atriums, and a large dining room whose walls were paneled in red. Along one wall were a series of paintings showing cupids throwing stones, selling flowers and perfume, racing chariots, gathering grapes, and washing cloth. There were scenes depicting famous couples from mythology and figures of the gods.

The garden contained fountains fed by water that flowed through lead pipes. Bushes were pruned into elaborate shapes, and there was space to relax indoors and outdoors.

The names of many of the other homes uncovered in Pompeii reflect unique artwork or mosaics found inside the ruins. There is the House of the Small Fountain, which is located next to the House of the Large Fountain. There is the House of the Anchor and the House of the Bear, named for mosaics found at the homes' entrances. The House of the Gilded Cupids and the House of the Silver Wedding are both named for artwork found inside them. The House of the Hanging Balcony contained the first balcony archaeologists discovered in Pompeii's ruins.

There are smaller homes, too, such as the House of Lucretius Fronto. But even the more modest homes contained something pleasing to the eye—mosaics, paintings or statues, or a garden with fountains. Pompeians appreciated the beauty of their surroundings and wanted spaces where they could enjoy it in public and in their own homes.

On that Day

It was August 24, A.D. 79. Pompeii was a city at peace, a city still under construction as workers continued the seemingly endless process of rebuilding structures damaged or destroyed in the earthquake 17 years earlier. But Pompeians were optimistic. They were rebuilding on a grand scale, re-creating homes and temples that were larger and more elaborate that the structures that had been there before. In the distance, Mount Vesuvius rose stately and elegant, its slopes covered with wildflowers and grasses. Pompeians likely did not even realize that they were living near a volcano. Vesuvius was simply a scenic mountain that added to the beauty of the region and helped provide exceptionally fertile soil.

In early August, the ground had begun to shake periodically, but few Pompeians were worried. The major earthquake that had severely damaged the city had taken place 17 years earlier, and these minor quakes seemed insignificant. A few statues may have fallen off their pedestals, cracks may have appeared in a few walls, but these seemed simply to be minor annoyances in a city that had seen far worse.

More troubling was the fact that several springs had stopped flowing with water and wells had dried up. Most Pompeians viewed these natural phenomena as signs that the gods were displeased with them, and those aware of the minor tremors and absence of water where it had once flowed increased their sacrifices in an effort to restore the gods' favor.

Had modern geologists existed in Pompeii's time, they could have warned the residents that, in fact, the disappearance of water was a far more troubling warning. The passages running deep below the earth into the crater of Mount Vesuvius were filling with vapor and gas. This, in turn, was causing a tremendous increase in the pressure on the layer of lava that formed the cap of the volcano.

By August 20, residents of Pompeii suddenly heard loud grumblings and roars from the vicinity of Vesuvius. Again, many believed that these were a sign of the gods' displeasure, but those residents old enough to remember the frightening roars that had preceded the earthquake of A.D. 62 may have begun to sense that there was cause for even greater alarm. Because only one-tenth of Pompeii's population is believed to have died in the eruption, it is likely that at least some of the people began to leave at this time, believing that an earthquake was about to strike the city.

The loud and frightening noise from deep in the earth was followed by more serious tremors, and then by unusually large waves forming in the bay. Animals, so often aware of pending natural dangers, suddenly seemed nervous and jittery. Cattle tried to break out of their stables. Dogs paced and whined. Large flocks of birds could be seen rising up from various perches and flying away from the city.

There were four days—four days of signs and warnings. Four days for the people of Pompeii to flee to safety. Tragically, few in Pompeii could accurately interpret these signs and understand the danger that was coming.

A DAY OF DARKNESS

It was early in the afternoon on August 24. People began their workday at dawn, and undoubtedly had been busy for several hours, when suddenly a deafening noise, something like a tremendously loud crack, came from the direction of Vesuvius. At the same time, the ground began to shake, harder and longer than it had done on any of the previous few days.

It had been a sunny August morning, but immediately the sky grew dark as night, and birds that had been flying overhead dropped, still and motionless, to the ground. Anyone able to see in the direction of Vesuvius would have noticed, according to Marcel Brion's *Pompeii and Herculaneum*, that the outline of the mountain had changed. The peak of Vesuvius seemed to have split, and then the terrified observers would have seen a far worse sight: a huge column of ash, cinders, and superheated rocks rising up into the sky.

Vesuvius had been dormant for so many years that Pompeians did not even know it was a volcano. Seismic activity seventeen years before the eruption, and in the four days leading up to it, was believed to be a sign of displeasure from the gods, not a signal of impending natural disaster.

The terrified Pompeians would have seen Vesuvius emitting what seemed to be a huge cloud of smoke. This cloud rose higher and higher, eventually reaching about 20 miles (32 km). It then began to spread out, forming into the shape of what one observer likened to an umbrella pine tree—a tree with a very long, narrow trunk beneath a spreading canopy of branches, not triangular like the classic Christmas-tree shape, but very wide at the bottom of the branches and gradually rounded above.

For approximately two hours the cloud rose and spread in the sky. Then, about 3:00 P.M., high in the earth's atmosphere, the cloud of ash began to cool. As it cooled, the cloud's contents began to rain down on the ground below.

The direction of the wind on that day made a fateful difference for Pompeii. Had it been blowing in the direction of the bay, much of the ash and stone would have fallen into the sea. On most days, the wind moved in this direction, from the north out to sea. But on August 24 the wind was moving inland across the Bay of Naples, and it carried the debris directly over Pompeii, 5 miles (8 km) away.

At first, what fell were small clumps of volcanic rock, called *lapilli*. Most of these were the size of pebbles, not enough to instantly kill; but undoubtedly these events were enough to alarm a significant portion of Pompeii's population, causing them to flee away from the city and either to the sea or to nearby towns.

Still, many Pompeians stayed behind—a decision that would cost them their lives. The rain of volcanic rocks continued for hours. Most of the population would have gone indoors, seeking shelter from this steady shower of stones. Inch after inch of lapilli began to build up on the roofs of Pompeii. Under the steady pressure of this ever-increasing weight, roofs began to collapse, trapping and killing those below.

At this point, many Pompeians began frantically to gather together loved ones, grab whatever coins or treasured possessions they could, and try to leave the city. The streets were crowded with frantic people and animals, all trying to move toward the city's gates, and movement was made more difficult by the rocks and stones raining down and clogging the roads. Night fell, and breathing became almost impossible as clouds of volcanic ash and dust settled everywhere.

DAWN AND DESTRUCTION

At dawn, the air finally began to clear. It must have seemed as if the worst was over for those still in Pompeii. People who had not yet left the city may have begun to emerge from the places where they had found shelter, the basements or buildings whose roofs had held up under the rain of volcanic debris. Others who, because of the crowds, had been unable to evacuate may have turned back and begun to head for their homes.

But shortly after dawn, a glowing river of superheated gas, ash, and debris (lava is actually a kind of melted liquid rock) roared out from Vesuvius and down the mountainside in the direction of Pompeii. Unlike some volcanic eruptions, this lava was traveling at a tremendous rate of speed, between 50 and 100 miles (80 and 161 km) per hour. It would have been completely impossible for anyone in Pompeii to outrun this deadly river, which swiftly poured through the streets of Pompeii.

The flow moved with such force that the walls that surrounded Pompeii, built to keep out an invading army, crumbled under the pressure. It swept through the city, killing everyone still there, some 2,000 people. They were buried under 12 feet (3.6 m) of fiery ash and pumice stones, and suffocated by air filled with ash so hot that it singed the victims' hair and burned the insides of their mouths.

Two more surges of lava shot out from Vesuvius and into Pompeii over the next few hours, but by then everyone in the city was dead. One day later, only the very tips of Pompeii's tallest buildings were visible. The rest of the city had been buried.

WHAT CAUSED THE ERUPTION?

The last eruption of Vesuvius had occurred nearly 2,000 years earlier, in prehistoric times before written records could have preserved the memories of those who survived. It is unlikely that anyone in Pompeii realized that they were living in the shadow of a volcano. In fact, this long period between volcanic eruptions contributed to the power of the devastating eruption that struck Pompeii.

Today we know far more about volcanoes and volcanic activity than the residents of Pompeii did. Volcanoes act like pressure valves on the earth's surface, releasing energy.

The earth's crust is divided into several large sections, which fit together much like the pieces of a jigsaw puzzle. These are called *tectonic plates*. Many of the active volcanoes on earth are located along the spots where these tectonic plates fit together. When the plates meet, they may rub together. This is the movement that triggers an earthquake.

At other times the plates may meet with enough force that a portion of one plate pushes itself under the other. The force and pressure of this movement causes the portion of the plate that has been pushed under the other to melt, transforming it into liquid rock, or magma. This magma is extremely hot; so hot that it creates gas and steam. The gas and steam build up in the passages far beneath the surface of the earth, creating so much pressure that eventually they find a weak spot in the surface of the earth and blast through. These "weak spots" are volcanoes.

There are many different sizes and shapes of volcanoes, but scientists have grouped them into three main categories: cinder cone, shield, and stratovolcano. Cinder cones are the smallest type of volcano, usually fewer than 1,000 feet (305 mters) high. They are shaped like cylinders with very steep sides. Formed by piles of ejected bits of rock, they tend to erupt lava from a gap in the side or base of the volcano, rather than the top. Examples can be found in Mexico (Parícutin) and Italy (Stromboli).

Shield volcanoes are the largest type, built from layers of fluid lava that flowed for a great distance before cooling. As a result, these types of volcanoes tend to be broader, spreading over greater distances, and have gently sloping sides. They tend to occur close to the water, often on islands. Hawaii's Mauna Loa is an example of a shield volcano, measuring 30 miles (48 km) wide and 60 miles (97 km) long.

Mount Vesuvius is an example of the third type of volcano, the stratovolcano. Stratovolcanoes are built from layer after layer of thick magma, and they are often extremely tall with steep sides. Stratovolcanoes are also usually the deadliest of the volcanoes, with the potential for very violent eruptions. Mount St. Helens, on the west coast of the United States, is another example of a stratovolcano.

Magma—liquid rock—collects deep below the surface of the earth in an area beneath the volcano known as the magma chamber. The magma is lighter than the rock around it, so it is continually trying to push upward. Above the magma chamber are layers of hardened rock, lava, and ash, but if enough gas and steam begin to accumulate beneath the surface of the earth the pressure increases, until the magma begins to shoot up out of the volcano through the central shaft. With sufficient pressure cracks can begin to split the side of the volcano, and magma will then shoot out of the sides or base of the volcano as well.

In some eruptions, this process can be slower, with lava gently oozing out of the top of the volcano in a steady gradual stream. But the eruption that struck Pompeii was what is now called a "plinian eruption," named after Pliny the Younger, a witness to the Vesuvius eruption who described what he saw in a letter to a friend.

In this eruption, Vesuvius was tightly capped in layer after layer of pumice rock. More and more pressure built up in the magma chamber, until it reached extreme levels—extreme enough to blow a hole through

The volcanic eruption started with a thunderous crack that was accompanied by a long earthquake. An ash cloud coming out of Vesuvius's crater would have darkened the August sky over Pompeii, terrifying the city's residents. Many people began to leave, and those that stayed behind faced certain death.

the thick rock, shooting volcanic debris miles into the sky. The loud roar that Pompeians heard was actually the sound of liquid rock shooting into the sky so quickly and with such force that it broke the sound barrier, triggering a sonic boom.

The ash, superheated rock, and cinders shot up into the sky in a giant column before spreading out. It was Pliny who described this cloud as resembling the shape of an umbrella pine tree. This shape has become one of the identifying features of a plinian eruption.

It is the moment when this cloud of volcanic debris begins to collapse that these eruptions become particularly deadly. This is not when the cloud seems to "rain" volcanic debris on the ground below but later, often several hours later, when the column itself collapses back into the volcano.

As the plinian column collapses, it triggers what is known as a *pyroclastic surge*. This is a boiling wave of volcanic debris that shoots out from the sides of the volcano. Huge clouds of powder and ash accompany this wave of molten rock as it races at speeds of up to 100 miles (161 km) per hour. The magma, even the air, would have been heated to 900°F (482°C) or higher.

The pyroclastic surge, devastating as it is to anyone within several miles of the volcano, is only the first step of what occurs when a plinian column collapses. As the solid ash and debris collapse back down into the volcano and reach the steam and gas below, they trigger a kind of volcanic storm, leading to rivers of mud flowing away from the volcano. Ash and other volcanic debris that may have fallen into nearby rivers and streams create additional mudflows, which can overflow riverbanks and move with great force into a surrounding area, flooding a region with mud. Ash can linger in the water long after the volcano has erupted, triggering mudflows days or even weeks later.

The victims in Pompeii in the hours, minutes, and seconds before their death witnessed each of the classic stages of this plinian eruption. First, the blast of the initial explosion, as volcanic debris shot up into the air. Second, the fallout, as small stones rained down on the city from the cloud above. Third, the column collapse, as the clearing air was a sign that the plinian column was collapsing back into Vesuvius. Next, the surge, as lava pushed out with tremendous force from the sides of the volcano. Finally, the flow, as the clouds of ash and rivers of lava raced down and into the streets of Pompeii.

Witness to History

Much of what we know about the people and buildings of Pompeii is a result of painstaking work by archaeologists, who have in the last few centuries labored to uncover the city and study the evidence preserved in the ash.

But we also know quite a bit about the explosion itself—what it looked like, the impact it had on those who saw it, even some clues about why certain people perished in the explosion while others did not. This is because of the writing of a 17-year-old man who watched the explosion from across the bay and whose uncle perished while attempting to rescue those living near the volcano.

At the time of the explosion, the Roman military had stationed a fleet at the Cape of Misineum, almost directly across the Bay of Naples from Vesuvius and slightly north and west of Pompeii. This fleet was under the command of Gaius Plinius Secundus, known as Pliny, or more accurately Pliny the Elder to distinguish him from his nephew, Pliny the Younger. Pliny the Elder was not only a military officer but also a scholar. His father, a wealthy member of the equestrian class, had provided his son with plenty of opportunities to study. Born near modern Como, Italy, about the year A.D. 23, he eventually came to Rome, where he became interested in nature and natural phenomena. He joined the military when he was about 21, and became an officer in the prestigious cavalry, leading successful campaigns along the Rhine River, in what is today Germany.

In addition to his career in the military, Pliny the Elder wrote several books, which earned him a reputation as a scholar and naturalist. His first book was a short study on the techniques for throwing spears from horseback. It is likely that he observed this combat style when fighting Germanic warriors. The book has not survived to modern times. Pliny's second book, written only a few years later, was *The Life of Pomponius Secondus*. Pomponius was one of Pliny's teachers and mentors; he probably wrote it as a tribute to his teacher after the man's death. Scholars are particularly intrigued with this second book, since it is one of the first known examples of biographical writing from the Roman age.

For his next writing he again found inspiration in his military campaigns along the Rhine River. The massive *History of the Germanic Wars* filled 20 volumes. His nephew later noted that the encyclopedic work was inspired by a dream in which his uncle was visited by the spirit of one of the military commanders who had perished during the wars and begged Pliny the Elder to ensure that he was not forgotten.

Pliny the Elder returned to Rome when he was in his mid-thirties. Like many military officers, Pliny was dependent on the goodwill of his commander in chief, in this case the emperor. Pliny had been serving under Emperor Claudius, who had supported and encouraged historians and scholars, but as Pliny moved into his late thirties Claudius died and the new emperor, Nero, preferred music and singing to serious scholarship. Pliny decided to give up any ambitions he may have had to become a senator, as many men of his wealth and stature would have done, but instead dedicated himself to writing. He produced three additional books during this time.

PLINY THE YOUNGER

By the year A.D. 62, Pliny the Elder had become an uncle. His sister had given birth to a son, named Gaius Caecilius Secundus. The boy's father died soon after he was born, and Pliny the Elder (who had no wife or children of his own) became the guardian of his nephew. In keeping with Roman custom, the young boy then took his uncle's name, and became Gaius Plinius Caecilius Secundus or, as we know him today, Pliny the Younger.

Pliny the Younger lived and was educated in his uncle's home in Rome. The elder Pliny was soon traveling again. After a civil war a new emperor, Vespasian, seized power; he was the father of a close friend of Pliny's. With a friendly emperor in power, Pliny the Elder's career once more took off,

Pliny the Younger wrote the only eyewitness account of Vesuvius's eruption, and managed to survive the natural disaster. His uncle, like many other victims, died from the noxious fumes spewed from the volcano's crater. Archaeologists later found these victims preserved under layers of ash and rock that covered the city.

and he held several positions that took him through much of the western part of the Roman Empire. Throughout this period, he spent time in areas we know today as France, Belgium, Spain, and northern Africa. At various times, Pliny the Elder was responsible for administering justice, handling the emperor's finances and personal possessions, and overseeing the taxation of the provinces.

Eventually, Pliny the Elder's career led him back to the military. He was appointed prefect of one of the two Roman navies, which was stationed at Misenum. From here, Pliny the Elder was responsible for overseeing the western half of the Mediterranean Sea. Despite the pressure of this position, he still found time to continue to write, producing the 37-volume *Natural History*, the work for which he is best known.

The *Natural History* contained an encyclopedic collection of all of the scientific and cultural knowledge Pliny had amassed throughout his life. "History" in this sense was intended not to mean events in the past, but rather "research." Published in A.D. 77, two years before Vesuvius's eruption, it was intended to offer a Roman perspective on science and culture, which up until that time had been based mainly on Greek study and interpretation. The volumes include research on astronomy and meteorology, geography, anthropology, and human physiology. There are volumes on birds, land animals, marine animals, and insects. There are six volumes dedicated to various types of trees, vines, and plants. Pliny explored how to run a farm, and dedicated several volumes to medicines that could be derived from plants and animals. These volumes are fascinating not only for their breadth and scope, but for the insight they give into the study of natural history during the Roman age.

Pliny the Younger was impressed by his uncle's ability to study, write, and still satisfy the demands of his political and military career. In a letter to a friend who was an admirer of Pliny the Elder's writing, the nephew explained that he began working before dawn, returning home around noon. After a light meal, he would then take some time to rest in the sun while someone read to him. He would periodically sit up to jot down a note or some quote from the material that was being read aloud. For the rest of the day he would alternate short periods of rest, during which a book would be read aloud to him or he would be dictating his own writing to someone else, with periods of intense study. He would often work in this way until one or two in the morning. He would take a break for a bath, but as soon as he emerged from the water, even while he was still drying off or receiving a massage, he would resume his habit of listening to a book or dictating one himself.

"A shorthand writer, with book and tablets, constantly attended him in his chariot," Pliny the Younger wrote, "who, in the winter, wore a particular sort of warm gloves, that the sharpness of the weather might not occasion any interruption to his studies; and for the same reason my uncle always used a sedan chair in Rome," so that every precious moment might be dedicated to study and his writing.

It was this extraordinarily curious man, obsessively interested in the mysteries of the natural world, who found himself stationed across the bay as Vesuvius roared into life. It is perhaps not surprising that the 56-year-old Pliny determined to get a closer look.

ACROSS THE BAY

Pliny the Younger and his mother were visiting his uncle at Misenum that August. It was Pliny's mother who first looked out over the water and noticed the frightening cloud, rising in the distance from across the bay. She alerted her brother, who had just enjoyed lunch and was busy with his studies. He quickly called for a servant to bring his sandals, then climbed up to a higher spot to get a better view.

The cloud was so far away that the observers knew only that it was coming from one of the mountains, but they did not immediately know that it was Vesuvius. Pliny the Younger was 17 at the time; he had never seen anything like this but, perhaps more alarmingly, neither had his uncle—who had traveled through much of the Roman Empire and studied all forms of natural phenomena. The cloud seemed to be white in places, and in others dark and spotted, as if it contained bits of earth. It shot up into the air in a straight column and then spread out like the branches of a tree.

The events that followed were described in great detail by Pliny the Younger in a letter to his friend Tacitus. They provide a key eyewitness account of the disaster that struck Pompeii.

Pliny the Elder quickly determined that whatever was causing the bizarre cloud was something important, something he wanted to observe more closely. As commander of the naval forces he had plenty of ships at his disposal, and he quickly gave the order for one of the smaller, faster ships to be prepared for him. He invited his nephew to go with him, but Pliny the Younger decided to stay. His uncle had given him a writing assignment, and he wanted to complete it before his uncle's return. This decision saved his life.

As the elder Pliny was preparing to board the ship, a messenger appeared with a letter from the wife of one of his friends. Her home was one of the villas dotting the coast much closer to Vesuvius, almost at the base of the mountain, and in the letter she begged Pliny to bring a ship and rescue her.

What had begun as a scientific expedition quickly became a rescue mission. Pliny the Elder instead ordered several large galleys (ships rowed by slaves) to be launched. He boarded the lead ship, determined to rescue not only his friend's wife but as many of the other coastal residents as possible. While those who were able were fleeing the frightening cloud, Pliny the Elder ordered his ships to be rowed directly toward it,

Darkness, unbearable heat, and a rain of ash and rock terrorized and doomed the people who lived near Vesuvius during the eruption. Those that did not, or could not, leave the area became preserved in a state of death. Above, the cast of a dog archaeologists believe was chained outside the House of Vesonius Primus during the natural disaster.

dictating his observations of what he saw to one of the scribes who were always with him.

"And now cinders, which grew thicker and hotter the nearer he approached, fell into the ships," Pliny the Younger writes, "then pumice-stones too, with stones blackened, scorched, and cracked by fire."

As they neared their planned rescue point, they realized that the water was no longer deep enough for them to sail into port. The falling debris of rocks and ashes had filled in the water closest to the shore, forcing back the bay and making it too shallow for the boat to approach the coast.

Apparently, Pliny the Elder now had to decide whether or not to turn back. The pilot on his boat urged him to return to Misenum and safety. But Pliny decided to press on. "Fortune favors the brave," he apparently said, and ordered the ships to sail toward the town of Stabiae. Stabiae was south of Pompeii and southeast of Vesuvius along the Bay of Naples. It was further from Vesuvius, and the home of one of Pliny's friends, Pomponianus. Pliny undoubtedly thought that, by sailing further from Vesuvius, he would be able to reach shore, rescue his friend and any others who needed assistance, and then sail back to Misenum.

Pliny was able to reach shore at Stabiae, and found his friend Pomponianus and members of his household in a complete panic. Pomponianus had already loaded many of his valuables onto ships, and was simply waiting for the wind, pushing inland in a southerly direction, to die down so that he could sail north to Misenum.

Upon arriving at his friend's home, Pliny decided to calm everyone down and wait for the wind to shift. Covered with bits of the ash that had rained down on the ship as he sailed past Vesuvius, Pliny asked to take a bath. He then encouraged everyone to sit down and have supper, eating with apparent ease and pleasure while the others picked at their food.

THE FIRES BEGIN TO BURN

Despite Pliny's seemingly relaxed approach to the bizarre phenomenon, members of Pomponianus's household could not help but notice that Mount Vesuvius was changing. It was now, according to Pliny the Younger, "blazing in several places with spreading and towering flames, whose brightness the darkness of the night set in high relief." The elder Pliny tried to soothe his hosts, telling them that the fires were simply from some country houses, abandoned by frightened people when the cloud of smoke appeared and left to burn until the entire house caught fire. Then he asked if he might rest for a while, and being taken to a guest room he promptly fell asleep, snoring loudly.

While Pliny slept, the rain of pumice stone and ash continued. The guest room he was using opened onto a courtyard, and gradually the courtyard began to fill with layer after layer of rocks. The others in the household had not been sleeping, and someone eventually realized that, if Pliny did not leave his room soon, the stones would completely seal it off. They woke him, and assisted him in climbing over the rocks to where Pomponianus and the others were debating what to do. Were they safer inside or outside?

A series of tremors that shook the house helped them to decide. The house tilted to the right and then the left, before returning unsteadily to its original position. They decided to brave the rain of pumice stones, and used towels to wrap pillows onto the top of their heads as protection from the falling rock.

It was now dawn, but outside it was as black as the darkest night. All around them were flares of light from torches and lamps as people frantically tried to decide where the safest place might be. Pliny led the others down to the shore, to see if they could possibly board the boats and sail away, but the waves were unusually high and choppy. The air was thick with ashes and volcanic debris.

Pliny sat down on a piece of old sail. Twice he asked for cold water and drank it. The air soon filled with a strong smell of sulfur, and the terrified observers could see what seemed to be flames in the distance. They began to run away; Pliny tried to stand up, but could not. Two young slaves attempted to help him, but he quickly fell back down, apparently struggling for breath and unable to move. The elder Pliny had often been short of breath in recent years; his nephew speculated that "some unusually gross vapour" emanating from the volcano had filled his lungs and made it impossible for him to breathe, and that this is what killed him.

Three days passed before those who had fled felt it was safe to return. When they did, they found Pliny the Elder where he had fallen, still fully clothed and without any marks or injuries on his body, seeming, as his nephew wrote, more like "a sleeping, rather than a dead man."

Those who ran from Vesuvius during the eruption had a slim chance of survival. The cloud of volcanic ash covered the nearby cities of Herculaneum and Stabiae, plunging the roads into darkness. Parents, children, and friends were separated during this time, as they struggled through earthquakes and falling pumice to reach safety.

WHAT PLINY THE YOUNGER SAW

This was the experience of Pliny the Elder, recorded by his nephew in a letter to a friend after witnesses who had survived returned to tell him of his uncle's final hours. In a second letter to the same friend, Tacitus, Pliny the Younger recorded his own personal experiences when Vesuvius erupted, noting the horrors and the uncertainty that accompanied this devastating event. It is important to remember that Misenum was much farther from Vesuvius than Pompeii. The frightening experience of Pliny the Younger was likely magnified the closer one was to the volcano.

After his uncle departed, Pliny the Younger returned to his studies, then bathed, ate dinner, and went to bed. But it was a largely sleepless night. He had grown accustomed to the minor earthquakes that had been common for the past few days, but that night they became increasingly violent. After a particularly fierce tremor, his mother came into his room and the two decided to move to the area of the house that overlooked the water. He tried to read, but was interrupted by a friend of his uncle's, who could not believe that, in the midst of an earthquake, the 17-year-old was reading while his mother sat nearby.

Finally, at the urging of his uncle's friend, Pliny and his mother decided to leave the house. It was close to six o'clock in the morning, but the sky was barely lit. Buildings were tottering on their foundations, and Pliny finally realized the danger they faced should one of the structures collapse on them. He and his mother decided to flee Misenum, and they soon found themselves caught up in a crowd, all heading in the same direction.

They moved away from the houses and toward the stables, but discovered that the chariots were sliding back and forth on the ground. The earth tremors were making it impossible to keep the chariots steady, even when servants attempted to place rocks around the wheels to hold them still.

Looking toward the water, they saw an even more frightening sight—the water had been pulled far back from the shore and there, on the suddenly expanded beach, were large numbers of fish apparently trapped on the sand. It was the same kind of natural warning that preceded the devastating tsunami that struck Southeast Asia in December 2004. Across the water, Pliny the Younger writes, "a black and dreadful cloud bursting out in gusts of igneous serpentine vapor now and again yawned open to reveal long fantastic flames, resembling flashes of lightning but much larger."

At this point, his uncle's friend warned them that their uncle, if he was alive, would want them to save themselves. He then hurried away, as the cloud of ash began to fall from the sky. Pliny's mother began to panic, urging him to save himself since he undoubtedly could run faster than she could. Pliny instead grabbed her hand, and dragged her with him.

He headed for the fields nearby, concerned that they would be crushed either by falling buildings or the mobs in the street. As they moved toward the fields, he writes, they were suddenly plunged into darkness, "not like that of a moonless or cloudy night, but of a room when it is shut up and the lamp put out. You could hear the shrieks of women, the crying of children, and the shouts of men; some were seeking their children, others their parents, others their wives or husbands."

It was all darkness and voices crying out around them for some time. Some mourned what was happening to them, or the loss of a loved one. Some called out for death, seeking an end to the terrifying experiences.

AN EYEWITNESS ACCOUNT

Many of the details we know about the eruption of Mount Vesuvius are the result of the letters of Pliny the Younger to Cornelius Tacitus, in which he recorded what he knew about his uncle's doomed voyage and his experience under the cloud of volcanic ash. The excerpt below, translated from the Latin, is taken from one of these letters:

Soon afterwards the cloud I have described began to descend upon the earth, and cover the sea. . . . My mother now began to beseech, exhort, and command me to escape as best I might; a young man could do it; she, burdened with age and corpulency, would die easy if only she had not caused my death. I replied, I would not be saved without her, and taking her by the hand, I hurried her on. She complies reluctantly and not without reproaching herself for retarding me. Ashes now fall upon us, though as yet in no great quantity. I looked behind me; gross darkness pressed upon our rear, and came rolling over the land after us like a torrent. I proposed while we yet could see to turn aside, lest we should be knocked down in the road by the crowd that followed us and trampled to death in the dark. We had scarce sat down when darkness overspread us, not like that of a moonless or cloudy night, but of a room when it is shut up, and the lamp put out. You could hear the shrieks of women, the crying of children, and the shouts of men; some were seeking their children, others their parents, others their wives or husbands, and only distinguishing them by their voices; one lamenting his own fate, another that of his family; some praying to die, from the very fear of dying; many lifting their hands to the gods; but the greater part imaging that there were no gods left anywhere, and that the last and eternal night was come upon the world.

[Source: Pliny, *Letters*, Vol. 1, Book 6: 20, Macmillan, 1923, pp. 493–495]

Some prayed to the gods, while others called out that there were no gods left and that this was the end of the world.

They could gradually see the darkness clearing in the distance, and then realized that it was flames. The flames stayed at a distance, and then again darkness came and another shower of ashes. The ashes were so thick and heavy that they had to continually stand up and brush them off, fearing that they might be buried under their weight. Pliny writes that he believed at this moment that he, and all the world, was dying.

Gradually, the darkness began to lift, and the cloud of ashes began to lessen. It finally seemed to drift away like smoke, and the sun could be seen in the sky, but only faintly, as if on a very hazy day.

What Pliny saw was a barely recognizable landscape, buried under a thick layer of volcanic debris. "Every object that presented itself to our yet affrighted gaze was changed," he writes, "cover'd over with a drift of ashes, as with snow."

This was the terrifying experience of one who survived that fateful eruption on August 24, 79. Pliny the Younger was in Misenum, 20 miles (32 km) from Pompeii. According to Marcel Brion, ashes and bits of volcanic rock rained down as far away as Rome, some 150 miles (241 km) from Pompeii.

Uncovering
the Ruins

Pompeii remained a town practically forgotten, a town buried under the ashes, for more than 1,600 years. Pompeii was not the only victim of Vesuvius that lay buried. Located 3 miles (5 km) east of Vesuvius at the time of the eruption was the resort town of Herculaneum, a smaller town than Pompeii (population about 5,000), known for its collection of luxurious villas and gardens overlooking the Bay of Naples. It is possible that Herculaneum was Pliny the Elder's initial destination when he was attempting to rescue the wife of his friend, the port he was unable to reach when falling volcanic rock and cinders filled the waters, making it too shallow for Pliny's boat to navigate.

Herculaneum was also destroyed when Vesuvius erupted, but the experiences of the two towns were quite different, evidence of the vast and varied forms of destruction caused by the volcano. While Pompeii was 5 miles (8 km) southeast of Vesuvius, Herculaneum was closer—only 3 miles (5 km)—but slightly northwest of the volcano. Because of the movement of the wind on August 24, 79, Herculaneum was upwind of the volcano when it erupted. As a result, initially the greater amount of rocks and ash fell on Pompeii.

Still, the giant cloud of volcanic debris reaching into the sky at such a close distance was extremely alarming to the people of Herculaneum. Ash was falling on their homes, although probably less than 1 inch (2.5 cm), during the course of the first few hours of the eruption. Most of the people of Herculaneum rushed to the beaches, loading their belongings onto boats or waiting for additional boats to come to their rescue.

Shortly after 1:00 A.M. on August 25, the volcanic cloud collapsed, triggering the first pyroclastic surge. This surge forced a violent rush of superheated gas and ash out the side and base of Vesuvius in the direction of Herculaneum. Hundreds of people had gathered in front of 12 boat-houses next to the water, awaiting rescue. They were killed instantly in the blast, which struck them at temperatures about 900°F (482°C). Their flesh and clothing were instantly vaporized in the intense heat. A separate flow of hot ash, rock, and pumice then buried the town.

There were several surges that followed over the next few hours. Shortly after dawn, one of these separate surges struck and buried the inhabitants of Pompeii.

In the days after the eruption, the landscape had changed completely. Those who had survived, who returned hoping to reclaim their homes and possessions, found that everything had vanished. Vesuvius was marked with long cracks and openings along its side and base, and steam and gas still rose up from those cavities. The air smelled of smoke, and bits of ash still floated in the air. The fertile green hills were now brown and gray, covered with layers of black, hardened lava. There were no more houses, no more temples.

A few of the former residents undoubtedly tried to find traces of their homes, bringing tools and shovels to try to dig in the places where they knew their homes had once stood. But if they were able to chip away bits of the hardened lava, toxic gases rose up from the cracks. What they did not know is that their primitive tools had little hope of excavating their town. While Pompeii was buried under 12 feet (3.7 m) of hardened volcanic rock, Herculaneum was buried under 65 feet (20 m) of volcanic debris. So the survivors settled in other places, and Pompeii and Herculaneum were little more than names that scholars found in certain documents from the Roman era.

DIGGING A WELL

One of the benefits of volcanic soil is that, over hundreds of years, it becomes extremely fertile, and gradually a town sprang up once more, a town that, no one knew, was placed directly above the remains of what had once been Herculaneum. This town was called Resina. It was not until the early part of the 1700s, sometime around 1710, that the first clues emerged of a town buried many feet below.

It began when a farmer in Resina was attempting to deepen the well on his land. The well had recently dried up, and he wanted to dig deeper to try to rediscover water. He dug deeper and deeper, until he struck not water but marble.

This was a happy discovery for the farmer. He was not concerned with any archaeological significance of what he had found in his well. Instead, he knew that sculptors paid well for good-quality marble, and so he decided to try to sell the marble he had uncovered to the nearest sculptor he could find.

Not far from Resina, an Austrian prince, Maurice de Lorraine, Prince of Elbeuf, was in the process of building a magnificent villa. Word of the farmer's discovery reached the prince—the farmer may have approached him or one of his workmen about selling some of the marble he had uncovered. The prince inspected the marble, and he realized that the pieces must have come from some impressive ancient structure. Like the farmer, the prince was not initially interested in the archaeological significance of the discovery; he was far more interested in obtaining unique and impressive marble pieces to decorate his villa.

The prince agreed to purchase the pieces the farmer had uncovered, and then he bought the farmer's land, hired his own workmen, and directed them to begin excavating the ground around the well in search of additional treasures. What they gradually uncovered was Herculaneum's theater, probably the most luxurious structure in the town, decorated with countless statues, vases, and candelabra. The workmen's task was not to preserve historic structures—it was to find treasure, and under the prince's direction they bored into the theater, not worrying about any damage they might be doing.

They ripped out bronze and stone statues. They pulled up marble vases and marble pillars. No effort was made to note where the objects were placed, or how deeply they were buried in the volcanic rock, as modern archaeologists would do. Instead, the workmen dug and dug. Many of the treasures were added to the prince's private collection. A few were presented by him as gifts to friends, including three magnificent statues of Greek women, which most likely had once adorned a portion of the theater of Herculaneum and were sent by the prince to his friend Prince Eugène in Vienna. Finally, when the prince had extracted all the treasures he thought he could find from the site, and facing protest from several in

Rome—including the pope—who were alarmed at so many ancient treasures falling into Austrian hands, this initial dig came to an end.

It was another foreign nobleman, building another elaborate home along the Italian coast, who again sparked interest in the treasures buried beneath the Resina soil. Charles III, the Bourbon monarch who ruled Naples, Sicily, and eventually Spain, was in the process of building a magnificent summer palace near Naples around 1738 when he first heard rumors of what the Austrian prince had dug out of the ground decades earlier. He sent a colonel from his army, Rocque Joachin de Alcubierre, to investigate.

Alcubierre was determined to also find treasure to adorn his king's palace. He ordered crews to resume digging at the site of the theater, and soon tunnels were spreading out throughout the site of what had

The first private excavation in Resina, the former site of Herculaneum, revealed artifacts and statues of an ancient town, and officials began to wonder about neighboring sites. The search for evidence of these ancient towns went on for several centuries. Above, a 1929 archaeological excavation of Pompeii.

CHARLES III

King Charles III was one of the earliest to sponsor the excavations of Pompeii. His aim was to discover ancient treasures to decorate his palace in Naples.

Charles III, the son of King Philip V of Spain and Isabella of Parma, was born in 1716 in Madrid. He was born to the king's second wife; the king already had two sons with his first wife, so there was little chance that Charles would inherit the Spanish throne. Instead, his mother ensured that he was named Duke of Parma, her homeland. By 1736, Charles took advantage of political unrest and war to claim the thrones of Naples and Sicily and have himself named king.

By most accounts he was a popular ruler, and for the next few years he enjoyed a period of prosperity in his palace in Naples, where treasures pulled from the ruins of Pompeii were brought to please him and to decorate his lavish home. In 1738, he married Maria Amalia of Saxony; they eventually had five daughters and three sons.

Charles III's father, Philip, died in 1746. His eldest son died before him, and so it was his second son, Ferdinand VI, who became king of Spain. He ruled for 13 years before dying; because he was childless he left no heir to claim the throne of Spain. The next in line was Charles III, and he became king of Spain in 1759 at the age of 43. Once he became the Spanish monarch, he decided to abdicate the monarchy of Naples, stepping down and naming his youngest son, Ferdinand, the new king of Naples.

Charles III ruled Spain from 1759 to 1788. During that period he took steps to consolidate the power of the monarchy and to strengthen and modernize Spain's military. Ill-fated attempts to cement Spain's position as a colonial power led to a disastrous alliance with France in the Seven Years War with England and secret efforts to aid the American colonies in their war for independence. During this period Spain lost and then regained Florida.

He died in 1788, and was succeeded by his second son, Charles IV.

once been Herculaneum. They uncovered frescoes and paintings on the walls of buildings, more statues, more marble carvings. The paintings and frescoes were chipped out of the walls to be carted off to Charles III's palace in Naples. Marcel Brion notes that Alcubierre's haste to provide his king with treasures was so intense that, in one case, he ordered an inscription of bronze letters encased in marble to be torn out, letter by letter, without making any attempt to first read the inscription. Once more Herculaneum was plundered, its ruins damaged, and its treasures carted away.

IN SEARCH OF MORE TREASURE

By 1748, Alcubierre had learned that there might be another buried city nearby, one with additional treasures that could be removed for Charles III. Alcubierre decided to see if the fresh site could yield any new treasure. He hired 24 diggers, 12 of whom were convicts, and on March 23, 1748, they began to dig above a spot that eventually proved to be the site of Pompeii's Temple of the Fortuna Augusta (Temple of Good Fortune). It was a temple adorned with statues and other treasures presented by Pompeians to earn good fortune from the gods, and Alcubierre was quickly encouraged. Clearly there was treasure to be found in this new site, and its excavation was much easier, since Pompeii was buried under a thinner layer of volcanic rock than Herculaneum.

There was no plan for this excavation, no effort to map the site as digging continued. Instead, Alcubierre simply ordered his men to start digging and, in a completely random way, they began boring down, throwing up the earth all around them as they dug, tearing paintings from frescoes, gathering up coins and other objects, and hauling them off to Charles III's palace. In some cases, once workmen had stripped all of the objects from a particular location they would then shovel earth back in on top of it.

By chance, several of the locations in Pompeii that the workers had randomly selected proved to be places where there were few great works of art to uncover, and for several years Pompeii was abandoned in favor of Herculaneum, which was thought to be a site far richer in treasure. It was not until December 1754 that workers, beginning to repair a road near what had once been one of Pompeii's gates (the Porta di Nuceria), uncovered what seemed to be tombs and the remains of a home. Alcubierre dispatched a team and oversaw a rapid digging at the site.

No one knew precisely what they were uncovering; it would not be for many years—not until August 20, 1763—that excavations uncovered an inscription reading, in Latin, "the commonwealth of Pompeians," and it was finally realized that the ruins belonged to that ancient Roman city. Excavation focused on areas where treasures were discovered, and was abandoned in areas where they seemed to be only ruins, but no valuable statues, coins, or frescoes. Nonetheless, several of Pompeii's important structures were uncovered, including the Great Theater in 1764, the gladiators' barracks in 1766, and the Temple of Isis in 1767. Gradually, the digging was joined by men who appreciated the historical significance of what they were uncovering, including Karl Weber and Francesco La Vega, who began to make drawings of the buildings as they were uncovered and also recorded details of each discovery in a journal.

From 1806 to 1815, much of the area around Naples came under French control, and the French continued work at Pompeii, bringing a far more methodical approach to the excavation and a schedule designed to set aside specific periods for digging and for scholars and visitors to tour the site. (Previously, a "discovery" would be arranged to coincide with the arrival of an important visitor, and works of art would be reburied in order for them to be happily uncovered just at the moment that a distinguished guest was observing the scene.) The French also created a map for the excavation, working systematically from east to west, and, at times, employing more than 1,000 workers in the task of excavating Pompeii.

After 1815, when the region went back to Bourbon control, the more organized approach to uncovering Pompeii continued, but at a far slower pace. Wars fought to regain control of the area around Naples had depleted the kingdom's wealth, and there were few funds available for archaeological projects. It would not be until 1860 that much of the western portion of the city was uncovered.

FINDING VALUE IN THE PEOPLE

In the earliest excavation, digging had been done randomly—boring down with tunnels and seeing what happened to come into view. Later, under the French, the technique switched to trying to uncover the streets of Pompeii, and then moving along them to uncover houses and buildings from the ground up.

Like the volcanic eruptions before it, the natural disaster that devastated Pompeii and its neighboring cities was soon forgotten, and people began to resettle in the area. Approximately three million people live around Mount Vesuvius, despite the possibility of future volcanic activity.

By 1863, a new man was in charge of excavating Pompeii, and this was someone with archaeological expertise. Giuseppe Fiorelli would direct the excavation for 12 years, until 1875, and during that period he instituted a number of important changes in the way Pompeii was being uncovered.

First, he ensured that far more accurate records were kept of what was being uncovered, and more importantly where the objects were placed and how deeply they were buried. In many cases, if the objects were not in danger of damage or theft, he gave orders to leave them precisely where they were found. (He also placed stricter controls over who was hired to work at the site, to attempt to prevent objects from slipping away.) Next, he focused on instituting a more systematic approach to the removal of dirt and rubble. Pompeii, up until his arrival, had been a random collection of pits dug into the ground and heaps of dirt and volcanic rock. Under Fiorelli's direction, the dirt and rubble were carted away so that the shape of the ancient town could gradually be seen. Fiorelli also changed the way buildings were being uncovered. Rather than uncovering the street first and then working to clear a building from the ground level up, Fiorelli instructed his team to uncover buildings and structures from the top down. This provided greater protection to structures during the excavation, and it also enabled workers to more accurately record the positioning of objects as they dug down.

Perhaps most importantly, it was Fiorelli who recognized the value of preserving the human victims of Pompeii. When they had fallen, these people had been buried in volcanic ash. Gradually, as more than a century passed, the human remains had decayed, leaving behind in the ash a hole perfectly outlining their shape and posture. Fiorelli developed the idea of filling these holes with plaster as they were uncovered, allowing the plaster to harden and form a cast. Gradually, the people of Pompeii—curled up in fear, attempting to protect themselves from the falling ash with a cloak or hood, clutching on to loved ones—took shape in the midst of the ash.

Fiorelli was followed by others, men such as Vittorio Spinazzola, who oversaw the excavation and reconstruction of many of the homes and shops along the Via dell'Abbondanza, and Amadeo Maiuri, who uncovered the walls around Pompeii and also made efforts to uncover portions of the city that predated A.D. 79 in an effort to learn about the very earliest occupants of Pompeii. Depending on the motives of those in charge and the finances available, excavation of Pompeii focused more on uncovering new structures and treasures or on restoring buildings already uncovered.

The uncovering of Pompeii continues to this day. There are substantial portions of the city's northern and eastern sections that are still buried. Some scientists support the idea of leaving portions of the city buried under the volcanic debris in order to provide an opportunity to study and observe the effects of volcanic eruptions.

POMPEII TODAY

Had Pompeii met the fate of other cities of the Roman Empire, it would have evolved and grown over the centuries. Old structures would have been replaced with new. Artwork would have been plundered or divided among descendants. Roads would have been widened. The city might have evolved into an agricultural and fishing town or a glittering resort with mansions dotting the landscape or a small, relatively prosperous city. These were all identities Pompeii enjoyed at various times in its history,

Recognizing the value of Pompeii, the Italian government implemented efforts to preserve the site and its artifacts and opened up the ancient city to tourists. Open to the public all year, Pompeii draws in thousands of visitors and helps support the local economy.

and it is likely that it would have assumed one of them again over the centuries. Traces of its past would have vanished over time.

But because of that eruption in A.D. 79, Pompeii remained frozen, perfectly preserved for centuries, its buildings forever captured as they were in that long-ago time, offering scholars and tourists a glimpse at what life was like in the Roman Empire. The streets paved with stones, the courtyards dotted with fountains and statues, the workshops and homes, still show traces of what was there more than 1,900 years ago. Despite the often shoddy methods first used to uncover the city, Pompeii continues in its role as an example of a prosperous, middle-class, first-century city under Roman rule.

Tourists can walk its streets. They can see the remains of the Amphitheater where gladiators once fought, visit the ruins of a temple where worshipers brought offerings to their favorite gods, or appreciate the quiet beauty of a green space a home owner carved out just steps from bustling shops. More than 2 million people walk the ancient streets each year. A bustling area catering to tourists, offering restaurants and hotels, has sprung up on the outskirts of the ruins, in the section known as the "new city."

People still live in the shadow of Mount Vesuvius—approximately 3 million people—for the same reasons they always have. The layers of volcanic rock have yielded rich and fertile soil. The area near the Bay of Naples is spectacularly beautiful. Fishing and farming produce plentiful results. And tourism now provides a new source of revenue and new opportunities to make money.

But Vesuvius has not been silent over the years. It continues to erupt periodically—its last eruption was in 1944—although these eruptions lacked the fury and devastation of the eruption that buried Pompeii.

This worries scientists, many of whom regard Vesuvius as one of the world's most dangerous volcanoes. Geologic records show that Vesuvius has erupted in the kind of devastating plinian eruption that struck Pompeii at fairly regular intervals over time. According to a report in *National Geographic*, these devastating eruptions occurred 25,000 years ago, 22,500 years ago, 17,000 years ago, 15,000 years ago, 11,400 years ago, 8,000 years ago, 3,780 years ago, and the Pompeii eruption nearly 2,000 years ago. Michael Sheridan, a volcanologist at the State University of New York at Buffalo, predicts that there is a greater than 50 percent chance of a major eruption from Vesuvius now, with the odds increasing ever so slightly each year. Residents who live near Vesuvius report feeling minor tremors periodically, but, like the people of Pompeii, they have become accustomed to them.

Chronology

1780 B.C.	Massive eruption of Mount Vesuvius buries settlements near modern-day Avellino, Italy.
c. 800 B.C.	Oscans build a settlement that they call "Pompeii."
474 B.C.	Greeks seize control of Pompeii, fortifying its defenses and building walls around the city.
310 B.C.	First unsuccessful attempt of Rome to conquer Pompeii.
290 B.C.	Pompeii seized by Rome; becomes "ally."
90 B.C.	Pompeii joins forces with other allies to overthrow Roman rule in the Social Wars.
89 B.C.	Roman general Sulla reestablishes control over Pompeii; people granted Roman citizenship.
62 A.D.	Earthquake strikes Pompeii; many buildings are damaged or destroyed.
79 A.D.	Mount Vesuvius erupts on August 24; within 24 hours Pompeii and nearby Herculaneum are buried.
c. 1710 A.D.	Farmer in Resina uncovers marble from Herculaneum while digging a well; Prince Elbeuf of Austria begins plundering the site of treasures.
1738	King Charles III of Naples and Sicily dispatches a new team to dig at the Herculaenum site to provide his palace with artifacts.
1748	Charles III's workers discover the Pompeii site.
1763	Workers uncover inscription identifying the site as the buried city of Pompeii.

1806   With French workers leading the excavation, a
        more systematic approach is introduced.

1863   Giuseppe Fiorelli introduces new techniques for
        excavating the site and recording what is discov-
        ered, as well as creating plaster casts from the

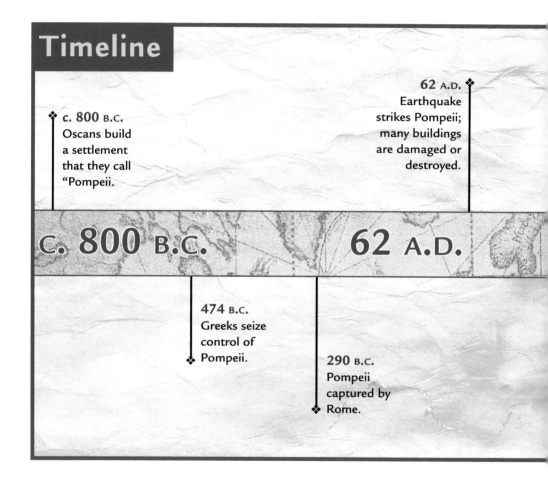

Timeline

❖ **c. 800 B.C.**
Oscans build
a settlement
that they call
"Pompeii.

62 A.D. ❖
Earthquake
strikes Pompeii;
many buildings
are damaged or
destroyed.

C. 800 B.C.   **62 A.D.**

474 B.C.
Greeks seize
control of
❖ Pompeii.

290 B.C.
Pompeii
captured by
❖ Rome.

spaces where humans, plants, and animals were trapped in the volcanic rock.

1944   Most recent eruption of Mount Vesuvius.

2010   More than 2 million tourists visit the ruins of Pompeii.

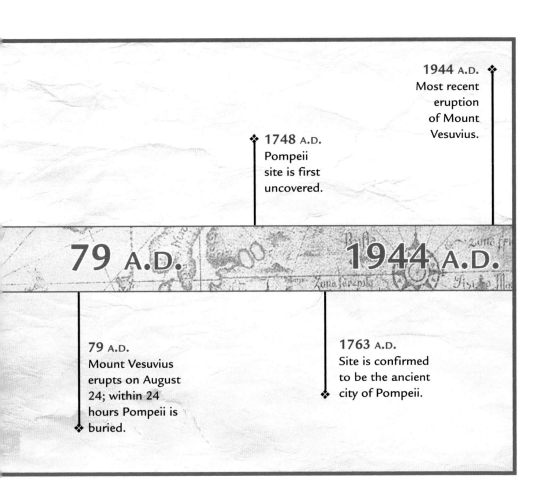

1944 A.D. ❖
Most recent
eruption
of Mount
Vesuvius.

❖ 1748 A.D.
Pompeii
site is first
uncovered.

79 A.D.   1944 A.D.

79 A.D.
Mount Vesuvius
erupts on August
24; within 24
hours Pompeii is
❖ buried.

1763 A.D.
Site is confirmed
to be the ancient
❖ city of Pompeii.

Glossary

Aediles   Elected officials in Pompeii responsible for streets, buildings, and markets.

atriensis   A servant who was the doorman and caretaker of a home.

caupona   A tavern or inn.

cena   The main meal of the day, served in the late afternoon.

Comitium   The place where elections were held.

Duumviri Iuri Dicundo   Two elected officials responsible for administering laws.

fibula   A brooch worn at the shoulder by men and women, used to fasten garments like the toga.

forum   A large public space surrounded by public buildings.

fullonica   A laundry service that bleached garments like togas and offered pressing and dyeing.

garum   A sauce made from fish.

gens pompeiana   People of Pompeii; the name used by Oscans who settled the region around the eighth century b.c.

lapilli   Small clumps of volcanic rock.

lararium   Household shrine to the gods.

magma   Liquid rock.

palestra   A Greek term for a public space for athletic competitions.

pistrinum   A mill and bakery.

popinae   Places where poorer Pompeians could buy meats left over from animal sacrifices.

pyroclastic surge   Boiling wave of volcanic debris that shoots out of the sides or base of a volcano.

Quinquennales   Public officials responsible for counting the population.

retiarii   "Net men"; gladiators equipped with nets and tridents used for combat.

tectonic plates   Large sections that mark divisions in the earth's crust.

thermopolium   A kind of café that sold hot drinks.

Bibliography

Beard, Mary. *The Fires of Vesuvius: Pompeii Lost and Found.* Cambridge, Mass.: Harvard University Press, 2008.

Bisel, Sara C. *The Secrets of Vesuvius.* New York: Scholastic, 1990.

Brilliant, Richard. *Pompeii AD 79.* New York: Clarkson Potter, 1979.

Brion, Marcel. *Pompeii and Herculaneum: The Glory and the Grief.* London: Elek Books, 1960.

Carpiceci, Alberto C. *Pompeii: 2000 Years Ago and Today.* Florence, Italy: BET, 1997.

Ciarallo, Annamaria. *Gardens of Pompeii.* Los Angeles: J. Paul Getty Museum, 2001.

D'Ambrosio, Antonio. *Women and Beauty in Pompeii.* Los Angeles: J. Paul Getty Museum, 2001.

De Franciscis, Alfonso. *Pompeii: Monuments Past and Present.* Rome: Vision S.R.L., 1995.

Dyer, Thomas H., ed. *Pompeii: Its History, Buildings, and Antiquities.* London: George Bell & Sons, 1875.

"Graffiti from Pompeii," Pompeiana.org. Available online. URL: http://www.pompeiana.org/Resources/Ancient/Graffiti%20from%20Pompeii.htm.

"Graffiti—The Urban Artists of Pompeii." Smithsonian Journeys. Available online. URL: http://www.smithsonianjourneys.org/blog/blog/2010/09/30/graffiti-the-urban-artists-of-pompeii.

Grant, Michael, and Rachel Kitzinger, eds. *Civilization of the Ancient Mediterranean: Greece and Rome,* Vol. 1. New York: Charles Scribner's Sons, 1988.

"The Herculaneum Women and the Origins of Archaeology," The J. Paul Getty Museum. Available online. URL: http://www.getty.edu/art/exhibitions/herculaneum_women.

James, Simon. *Ancient Rome.* New York: Dorling Kindersley, 2000.

Kraus, Theodor. *Pompeii and Herculaneum: The Living Cities of the Dead.* New York: Harry N. Abrams, 1973.

Lendering, Jona. "Pliny the Elder," Livius. Available online. URL: http://www.livius.org/pi-pm/pliny/pliny_e.html.

Maiuri, Amedeo. *Pompeian Wall Paintings.* Berne, Switzerland: Hallwag, 1960.

———. *Pompeii.* Novara, Italy: Istituto Geografico de Agostini, 1951.

Nappo, Salvatore Ciro. "Pompeii: It's Discovery and Preservation," BBC History. Available online. URL: http://www.bbc.co.uk/history/ancient/romans/pompeii_rediscovery_01.shtml.

Pellison, Maurice. *Roman Life in Pliny's Time*. Philadelphia: George W. Jacobs & Co., 1897.

Pliny. *Letters*. William Melmoth, trans. New York: Macmillan, 1923.

"Pompeii," Discovery Channel. Available online. URL: http://dsc.discovery. com/convergence/pompeii/pompeii.html.

"Pompeii and the Roman Villa," National Gallery of Art. Available online. URL: http://www.nga.gov/exhibitions/pompeiiinfo.shtm.

"The Samnite Wars," UNRV History. Available online. URL: http://www.unrv. com/empire/samnite-wars.php.

Starr, Chester G. *The Ancient Romans*. New York: Oxford University Press, 1971.

Stewart, Doug. "Resurrecting Pompeii." Smithsonian.com. Available online. URL: http://www.smithsonianmag.com/history-archaeology/pompeii. html?c=y&page=4.

Tanzer, Helen H. *The Common People of Pompeii: A Study of the Graffiti*. Baltimore: Johns Hopkins Press, 1939.

"Vesuvius Countdown," National Geographic. Available online. URL: http:// ngm.nationalgeographic.com/2007/09/vesuvius/vesuvius-text/7.

Zanker, Paul. *Pompeii: Public and Private Life*. Cambridge, Mass.: Harvard University Press, 1998.

Further Resources

Books

Bisel, Sara C. *The Secrets of Vesuvius*. New York: Scholastic, 1990.

Connolly, Peter. *Pompeii*. New York: Oxford University Press, 1994.

Deem, James M. *Bodies from the Ash: Life and Death in Ancient Pompeii*. New York: Houghton Mifflin, 2005.

James, Simon. *Ancient Rome*. New York: Dorling Kindersley, 2000.

Nardo, Don. *Life in Ancient Rome*. San Diego: Lucent Books, 1997.

Sonneborn, Lisa. *Pompeii*. Minneapolis: Twenty-First Century Books, 2008.

Web Sites

Pompeii: The Last Day
http://dsc.discovery.com/convergence/pompeii/pompeii.html
Interactive site by the Discovery Channel that explores the events of Pompeii and includes videos of volcanoes and details of ongoing excavations.

Pompeii
http://www.history.com/topics/pompeii
The History Channel's resource on Pompeii. Describes life in Pompeii, the eruption of Mount Vesuvius, and the reconstruction of the site.

Pompeii: Unraveling Ancient Mysteries
http://www.harcourtschool.com/activity/pompeii
Interactive site with details of Pompeii, Herculaneum, and Vesuvius, images of structures and artwork uncovered at Pompeii, and details of the eruption in A.D. 79.

Roman Empire in the First Century
http://www.pbs.org/empires/romans/
Provides information about the Roman Empire, life in the first century, an emperor game, and a quiz to determine which emperor you most resemble.

Vesuvius Volcano
http://www.gso.uri.edu/vesuvius/home/
University of Rhode Island site that teaches about volcanic activity by studying the eruption that buried Pompeii.

Picture Credits

Index

About the Author

HEATHER LEHR WAGNER is a writer and editor. She is the author of more than 40 books exploring historical, political, and social issues for middle-school and high-school readers. She earned a B.A. in political science from Duke University and an M.A. in government from the College of William and Mary.